The Museum Transformed

Douglas Davis

THE MUSEUM TRANSFORMED

DESIGN AND CULTURE IN THE POST-POMPIDOU AGE

Abbeville Press   Publishers   New York

Frontispiece:
Fumihiko Maki and Associates.
Spiral Building, Tokyo.
Detail of exterior.

Foreword translated by Carol Volk.

Editor: Constance Herndon
Production editor: Laura Lindgren
Designers: Karen Salsgiver
and Susan Carabetta
Production manager: Dana Cole

Note: All quotes from interviews that are
not otherwise credited have been supplied
by the author.

Library of Congress Cataloging-in-
Publication Data

Davis, Douglas, 1933–
     The museum transformed: design and
culture in the post-Pompidou age /
Douglas Davis.
          p.   cm.
     Includes bibliographical references.
     ISBN 1-55859-064-1
     1. Art museum architecture.
     2. Architecture and society.
     3. Architecture, Modern—20th
century.   I. Title.
     NA6695.D38   1990
     727'.7'0103—dc20   89-18227
                                           CIP

ISBN 1-55859-064-1

Printed and bound in Japan.
First edition.

CONTENTS

1
Piano and Rogers/
Richard Rogers
Partnership.
Pompidou Center,
Paris. View of
escalator and
courtyard below.

If it is true that access to art is one of the rights of humanity, extraordinary art must be made accessible to the largest numbers of people. For that we need museums that are themselves exciting to see, architectural works whose beauty compels us even as they efface themselves behind the beauty of the art. It is a difficult challenge, but one that great architects from Wright and Pei to Meier and Stirling have triumphantly met.

Over the last few decades, architects from every country and every perspective have profoundly altered the way we think about museums. Whether we speak of the adventurous Pompidou Center in Paris or the Mediathèque in Nîmes, New York's reformed Museum of Modern Art, Columbus, Ohio's brand new Wexner Center, or the Musée d'Orsay, installed in an old train station in Paris, the distinctive architecture of each has dramatically changed the way the public now thinks of the museum's role. Douglas Davis is entirely right when he argues that this evolution has made the task of designing the museum virtually "impossible," for the museum is no longer a staid, traditional architectural genre. In the best sense, each new museum is unpredictable, always formed on the basis of new expanding collections, exhibitions, and needs—needs defined by the public.

The extraordinary variety of museums, and the extraordinary variety *within* museums, has necessarily discouraged the dominance of a single style in the current proliferation of museum construction. The demands of a renovation are not those of a new building, for instance, nor can a collection of folk art be presented in the same manner as Cubist paintings or antique furnishings. An invisible thread nonetheless joins projects as varied as the Menil Foundation in Houston, the Spiral Building in Tokyo, and the Staatsgalerie in Stuttgart: the desire to make the collections as visible and readable as possible, and to provide the late-twentieth-century public with broad access to the shared treasure of its heritage.

This is not to suggest that nineteenth-century museums were poorly conceived. Supported by an educated, refined, although limited audience, they ordered, classified, and celebrated the artifacts of human civilization, thereby making humanity itself the object of study. If the museum has changed radically today it is primarily because the composition of its audience has expanded so dramatically. Yet the diversity of art works has also had a decisive effect, for art seems now to exceed the capacity for classification, overwhelming even the most learned experts. The belief that our knowledge and understanding of art is comprehensive is an illusion that may have suffered, but creativity and invention are now better represented. True respect for the public consists in allowing us to encounter the full and at times confusing range of artistic production, an encounter that is unique, precarious, and begins anew with each visit. By providing us with this experience, contemporary museums broaden our view of ourselves as well as our understanding of the visual world.

The greatest architects have created environments that nurture precisely this sense of the richness of human potential. A visit to the museums they have created ceases to be a chore or a cultural obligation and becomes instead a simple, joyful activity. By offering the possibility of a many-faceted experience that can be approached from a variety of angles and that responds to a range of interests, the contemporary museum has found a broad new public.

Which is also why the museum must offer cinemas, auditoriums, pleasant restaurants, rest areas, bookstores, boutiques, and gardens. Simply put, the museum must be receptive to the spirit and flesh of human beings. Only then can it truly become a place where we visit, find that we are sorry to leave, and depart restored. In order to see, we must want to look, to be able to linger, leave, return, hesitate, and return again.

Hidden between the lines of *Museum Impossible* is an idea I would like to put into my own words: art should be everywhere, at every moment, and in every place. We know this and through the creation of accessible palaces of culture we should work towards it. Yes, life has other dimensions—work, activity, pain, joy. But by bringing together rare and diverse experiences, the museum can give us an opportunity to focus on life in its most intense moments. The museum as it is defined in this book becomes a place of passage, a place to gather resources not available elsewhere, a place that enriches our lives. The modern or contemporary museum, isolated at once from the cloistered attitudes of the past and from the banal implications of mass media in our time, sends us back into the world of daily life, transformed.

Jack Lang
Minister of Culture
France

To J for water
To G and H for earth
To L and M for fire
To V for air
To K for breath

ACKNOWLEDGMENTS

My debts owed in exchange for this book, intellectual, professional, and personal, are endless. Among the tiny percentage I have the space to publicly acknowledge here are Thomas Messer, John Walsh, Thomas Krens, Henry Hopkins, Ryzard Stanisławski, Pontus Hulten, Richard Oldenberg, and Giuseppe Panza di Biumo, with whom I have discussed the situation of the museum for many years. Cesar Pelli, Richard Rogers, I. M. Pei, Emilio Ambasz, Arata Isozaki, Fumihiko Maki, O. M. Ungers, Philip Johnson, James Stewart Polshek, John Carl Warnecke, and Frank Gehry are simply a handful of the architects who have discussed the same subject with me, more than once, with intensity and generosity.

From first to last, Jane Bell has been steadfast in support and intellectual provocation. Mark Magowan, Sharon Gallagher, and Constance Herndon at Abbeville Press, as well as designer Karen Salsgiver and the late Luis Sanjuro, were critical managers of a complex project that required continual revisionism, if not reform.

Richard Lanier and the Asian Cultural Council made it possible for me to travel to Japan, where I was able to work and study in Tokyo at International House; while there I benefited enormously from the advice and guidance of Alexandra Munroe and Rand Castille. In its early stages, the book also received research support from the intern program at Cooper Union, most notably from Nina Hofer and Janine Roux. The Computer Lab at ArtCenter College has been equally vital, particularly in the very last stages. Finally, without Katrina Swendseid's research, ideas, and buoyant activism, *The Museum Transformed* would have been impossible.

Douglas Davis

Chapter One   THE MUSEUM IMPOSSIBLE

2
*West facade of
the Louvre, c. 1660.
Engraving by Israel
Sylvestre.
Louvre, Paris.*

In Which the Stage Is Set, the Theater Is Empty

The architect, by his arrangement of forms, realizes an order which is a pure creation of his spirit; by forms and shapes he affects our senses to an acute degree and provokes plastic emotions. . . . It is then that we experience the sense of beauty.
—Le Corbusier
"Towards a New Architecture: Guiding Principles," in L'Esprit Nouveau (1920)

Who can deny that until now the French people have been strangers to the arts, and that they have lived among them without participating in them? Painting or sculpture offer rare gifts; they become the conquest of a rich man who may have purchased them at a low price. Jealous of his exclusive possession, he admits only a few friends to share a sight forbidden the rest of society. Now at least by favoring the custom of public exhibition, the public, for a modest payment, shares a portion of the riches of genius; they may likewise come to know the arts, to which they are not as indifferent as they affect to believe; their understanding will increase, their taste be formed.
—Jacques-Louis David (1798), quoted in McClellan, "The Politics of Aesthetic Display" (1984)

Now a concept is the notion of a clearly determined group of things; its limits may be marked precisely. Emotion, on the contrary, is something essentially fluid and inconsistent. Its contagious influence spreads far beyond its point of origin, extending to everything about it, so that it is not possible to say where its power of propagation ends.
—Emile Durkheim and Marcel Mauss, Primitive Classification (1903)

If the artistic dream of this century has been purity, its nightmare has been the museum. From its earliest origins—which no one can precisely date—the palace of culture that Le Corbusier hoped to construct and Kazimir Malevich dreamed of perfecting has contradicted the monastic aims of its founders, its managers, and most of all its architects. Time and again the museum has burst its categorical limits, nearly always redefining its capacity and expanding its audience. In the beginning what we have come to call "museums" were circumscribed in intention and audience. History provides a long list of palaces and great houses that conserved and occasionally displayed rare treasures in a manner resembling our contemporary houses of culture. Ptolemy I referred to one of these palaces in ancient Alexandria as a *Mouseion*, comparing it to the legendary "realm of the muses," where the gods and goddesses of history, poetry, dance, and other arts meditated—perhaps the first in an ongoing series of doomed attempts to distance the museum from real, sordid life. In the fifteenth century Pope Sixtus IV stored his own collection in what came to be known as the Museo Capitolino. Throughout Europe, in Italy, in Germany, in France, many museumlike organisms sprang up during the Renaissance and the Enlightenment; often treasures were exhibited in private homes that were opened to visitors for limited periods of time. In England in 1683 Oxford University established the Ashmolean Museum to collect "rarities of art and science" as

3

3
Main facade of the Louvre, Paris, with partial view of I.M. Pei's pyramid.

educational tools. In 1753 Parliament established the British Museum to house the private collection of the monarch, perhaps the first art museum supported by public revenues.

But the critical psychic transition to a totally "public" institution with wider implications took place in Paris, in the wake of the French Revolution. Although its origins can be traced back to Louis XIV, the opening of the Louvre in 1793 was a thoroughly republican event, nourished at once by the Enlightenment and by democracy. Since then museums public and private have flourished throughout the world. It is impossible to say how many institutions devoted to the display of art, science, and other subjects have risen since the eighteenth century, but certainly tens of thousands, perhaps many tens of thousands. Aside from schools, stadia, centers of government, and religious structures, no building type can match the museum for symbolic or architectural importance. France's revolutionaries for instance, commonly referred to the Louvre as an institution dedicated to the glory of the nation. Precisely because we align our highest aspirations with the museum rather than the cathedral, the synagogue, or the shrine, we consistently neglect the social and political forces lurking just inside its gilded doors. But there is no way to analyze or interpret museums—much less their architecture—without taking these forces into account. From the first the Louvre was a creature of politics. In 1750 Louis XV had opened the smaller Luxembourg Gallery to the public to display ninety paintings from the royal collection, mainly to counter rumors that he had allowed France's treasures to deteriorate at Versailles. Almost forty years later the Revolution inspired the natural demand that all of the King's treasures be placed on public view: the decision to unveil his paintings and sculpture in the Louvre, a palace long the object of great national pride, was equally predictable.

The immediate controversies about renovation and installation were layered with ideological and historical implications. Many architects argued, suc-

cessfully, that the Louvre should not be crowded with luxurious royal furnishings in the manner of the Luxembourg; instead, bare walls and halls were required to focus the viewer's eye on the pictures. They also argued, unsuccessfully, that the Grande Galerie of the Louvre was too long (1,300 feet) and should be broken into smaller units or "rooms."

Many artists, historians, and politicians also wanted to use the newly renovated Louvre to destroy the old, corrupt master-apprentice system. By filling the gallery with masterpieces from every period and permitting young artists to educate themselves by copying them at their leisure, the revisionists hoped to arrest what they saw as the decline of French painting. But when the gallery opened on August 10, 1793, with an eclectic installation that mixed artists and styles indiscriminately, a phalanx of outraged artists, led by Jacques-Louis David, protested. Their protests were acknowledged when the Louvre invited them to revise the installation. Later, the once-royal, now-public collection was didactically rearranged again by periods and categories, rather like the neat arrangement of words and definitions in Diderot's *Encyclopédie*, the quintessential Enlightenment text. Matters of lighting and preservation were similarly inflected by the spirit of the period. The committees that governed the Louvre in the years after the Revolution chose to bathe the gallery in radiant natural light from above rather than from side windows, a decision proper for an age that relished clarity and rational inquiry. Paintings were to be restored to their original appearance, following facts rather than interpretation. Finally, young painters were allowed to copy the old masters from close, unobstructed access: seven days out of every ten, the paintings were hung at eye-level, without roped-off protection.

In spirit (if not always in execution) the postrevolutionary Louvre was thoroughly modern. Even the final decision— later reversed, of course—to leave the great long hall open rather than broken into smaller rooms or galleries anticipates museum design of this century. Rather than confine art in spaces the scale of pri-

4
Karl Friedrich Schinkel. Altes Museum, Berlin.

5
Ludwig Mies van der Rohe. New National Gallery, Berlin.

4

5

vate drawing rooms, David and his colleagues instinctively opted for open space and public access—for a vision of art as common property. Here, as always, a critical division arose between those who wished to enclose and therefore sanctify art and those who preferred open, flexible spaces. The early Louvre was committed to accessibility and education, not to decoration, not to preserving the "aura" of either the crown or of art itself. Since then, architects and their clients have sometimes allied themselves with one pole or the other and sometimes straddled both, but the distinction between these archetypal attitudes remains clear. Not long after the opening of the Louvre, the French theorist J. N. L. Durand published a paradigmatic design for a museum that merged the "open" and the "closed" museum but certainly favored the latter: Durand's ideal, constantly cited since then as a prototype,[1] combined a series of long, sequential galleries surrounding four courtyards and a rotunda. In many ways, Karl Friedrich Schinkel's magnificent Altes Museum in what is now East Berlin codified Durand's scheme in 1830, just as Ludwig Mies van der Rohe's National Gallery in West Berlin has come to represent—fairly or unfairly—wide-open modernity. Perched like a low, flat glass box on a steel podium, the visually undifferentiated space of the National Gallery opens itself irrationally to light. Simply to erect exhibitions its curators must invent and install walls and they must draw curtains across the transparent facade to protect the art from sun. Here in this one embattled city the museum divides itself and its supporters, some falling to the left, with Mies, some to the right, with Schinkel. The intensity with which Schinkel and Mies attacked these projects is equally symptomatic of the importance of the museum. More than the civic monument, the museum has become the architect's paramount vehicle of expression—his epic canvas, in effect. The notion that we can detect the critical qualities of talents like Frank

Lloyd Wright, I. M. Pei, Hans Hollein, or Fumihiko Maki (as well as Schinkel and Mies) in their museum designs is a staple of contemporary architectural criticism. Surely the cause of this is deeper simply than the advantages afforded by large budgets and great scale, advantages that are regularly attached to civic monuments or office buildings. No, it is the undeclared presumption that the exterior of a great museum should match its contents in terms of visual significance, and equally critical, in "signature"; the building, we think, should be as personal in its formulation as the painter's canvas or the draftsman's sketch. Certainly some of the most legible evidence of the uncompromising modern temper can be seen in Mies's National Gallery, in Corbusier's visionary drawings for a "Museum of Unlimited Growth," in Wright's Guggenheim Museum in New York, and in the technocratic trappings of the Pompidou Center in Paris, by Renzo Piano and Richard Rogers. What came to be known as "postmodernism" in the seventies and eighties depended heavily upon museum articulation—witness the Allen Memorial Art Museum addition in Oberlin, Ohio, by Robert Venturi and John Rauch (1976), the Staatsgalerie in Stuttgart by James Stirling (1984), and Michael Graves's several proposals for additions to the Whitney Museum of American Art in New York (first announced in 1986 and amended, often, later), all of which depended in their conception upon references to stylistic precedents. And of course with Richard Meier's decidedly striking High Museum in Atlanta the references, although modern rather than revivalist in the pure sense, are equally crucial.

Often museums of this character are assailed by traditionalists, most of all by curators, collectors, and artists, for their insensitivity to what is regarded as the cen-

tral purpose of these buildings—the serene, uninflected contemplation of works of art.[2] But neither clients nor public seem to agree. What they want and what they are getting, over and over, is an architectural form far more complex than that implied by the saintly connotations of the term *Mouseion*, a form that harbors lecture halls, theaters, restaurants, bookstores, and, on occasion, classrooms. Despite its unprecedented catholicity, this form is inherent in the historical evolution of this museumlike (not museum-pure) institution, which responds in our time to a public unimaginable to Ptolemy I, to Louis XV, or even to Diderot and David.

6

In Which the Ticket Window Opens, the Line Begins to Form

The word of ambition at the present day is Culture. Whilst all the world is in pursuit of power, and of wealth as a means of power, culture corrects the theory of success.
—*Ralph Waldo Emerson, "Culture" (1841)*

Massive numbers alone have altered the architecture of the museum. As the visitors have risen in numbers from dozens or hundreds in a day into thousands, the notion that the viewing gallery can retain the intimacy of a nobleman's drawing room, or even a king's salon, has grown increasingly absurd. In the United States, the model may have been humbler (the grand parlor of a J. P. Morgan or the living room of any bourgeois collector) but here, too, is an ideal that cannot withstand the impact of extraordinary crowds—rising, in the case of the Picasso retrospective at the Museum of Modern Art in 1980, to a crush of almost 7,400 per day and demanding the use of the same ticket agencies that serve baseball teams and Broadway theaters. The first appearance of the vulgar public—the art hordes—in the salons of Paris in the middle of the last century were chronicled by William Makepeace Thackeray in a memorable passage of journalism from 1848, when he complained of the "ugly hands" all around him, "hands that are hammering or weaving or filing all week." Yet the dream of sanctity remains, cherished even by MOMA itself—or rather the curator of the collection, William Rubin, who often railed in his long tenure against the corruption of meditative viewing, which he blamed on the architects who create what he clearly regarded as pleasure palaces.[3] The space Rubin chose for MOMA's collection, on the other hand, is simply a labyrinthine series of rooms linked to rooms, each modest in dimensions, windowless, without large-scale corridors, rather like an endless spiral of suburban living rooms.

But by and large American architects have rejected Rubin's ideal. The idea that the museum space has to be open and receptive, that it must serve many needs other than simply providing uninterrupted visual access to art, this is an idea that has primarily triumphed in the United States. Hardly a few yards beyond the outer core of William Rubin's closed-door installation, architect Cesar Pelli has provided a refutation of it with an ascending staircase fronting on a luxuriant garden displayed without benefit of frames or walls just beyond the visitor's eyes. Pelli's open and bustling escalator exemplifies the extent to which the American museum has become primarily public, shedding its private and royalist connotations. This is a constant theme in the evolution of the arts in the United States. Indeed the ideal of a "democratic culture" preceded the amassing of most great American collections, while the Louvre and many subsequent European museums sprang from royalist origin. "The American museum was and is an idea. The European museum was a fact," Nathaniel Burt forcefully explains. "Almost without exception the European museum was first a collection. With few exceptions most American museums were first an idea. . . ."[4] The American museum is also incurably didactic, which is no doubt the source of its overwhelming popularity at a moment in history when the

cathedral has lost its powerful pedagogic role. In his magnificent study *The Architecture of the City*, Aldo Rossi argues that monumentality in the urban context accrues only to those institutions that claim cultural and social power at once, a claim that in turn demands a declarative or figurative presence. Certainly the civic function of the museum in the United States, and increasingly in Europe and Asia, is based on the same didactic passion that led to the widespread establishment of public schools and universities—"the crusade," as Thomas Jefferson put it, "against ignorance." In virtually every American city, museums have been chartered or founded on principles similar to those of public education, a historical fact normally overlooked by critics, theorists, and curators.

At the same time we would be wrong to link the school or university to the museum in exact or pedantic terms. The museum audience is hardly the equivalent of a student body. Rather, it attends the museum voluntarily, rather like a leisured *bonhomme* in search of pleasure or learning as a liberal art. The Louis Harris studies of museum attendance from the early 1970s clarified this point and marked a seismic shift in our perception of the museum audience.[5] For the first time both museum professionals and the lay public learned that the once-recondite pleasures of viewing art were now shared by an audience that approached the size of the throngs that mob sports events and commercial films. Later studies conducted in the mid-1980s confirmed their continuing popularity. In a nation of almost 300 million citizens, the arts (performing as well as fine arts) have consistently polled an approval rating of between eighty-five and ninety-five percent for their fundamental importance to "the quality of life." Museum attendance itself has hovered around the 60 percent mark, according to the Harris reports, both in the 1970s and the 1980s. Subsequent studies by the Institute of Museum Services translated Harris's conclusions into the astonishing figure

of 300 million visits per year paid to museums.[6] Granting that the figures also showed that some visitors return often (forty-three percent of the population averages four visits per year), these and similar findings produced by the Harris surveys became a political and conceptual watershed. Immediately a series of investigations followed into the economic impact that museums, and indeed cultural activities of all kinds, have on their communities. (One, conducted by the New England Foundation for the Arts, concluded that the aggregate impact of known cultural organizations on the six northeastern states, both directly, in terms of salaries, and indirectly, in terms of tourism and consumer spending, reaches $1.5 billion each year.) No longer could politicians conveniently ignore appeals for assistance from institutions that had been considered the preoccupation of a wealthy minority. Nor could popular sociologists like Herbert Gans and Marshall McLuhan continue to maintain the credibility of a thesis that posited an unbridgeable gap between "high" and "low culture," a gap that they believed would inevitably widen, given the vulgarizing effect of television upon common men and women. "High" art, for Gans, McLuhan, and their many sympathizers, was the exclusive preserve of a small circle of "aficionados" (patrons, collectors, wealthy businessmen, and other artists). The "masses," to their mind, remained indifferent—until the statistical evidence (as well as the sensorial evidence of crowded museum halls) contradicted them.

Not that the Harris figures were beyond criticism or conclusive in any qualitative sense. Paul Dimaggio of Yale has attempted in a series of studies to modify and reinterpret the Harris polls, emphasizing education as the demographic link bringing visitors of varying ages, races, and income levels into the museum. Furthermore none of the quantitative Harris poll findings about attendance are necessarily static. In the United States the rapid increase in the number of women holding jobs began to lower museum attendance, as well as per capita leisure hours, by the mid-1980s, barely a decade after

the Harris studies began. With the addition of cable television, there are more hours of arts coverage than ever, including live coverage of concerts and performances, which may mean a further reduction in museum attendance. Although Harris concluded in a 1984 report that cable television subscribers seemed to be increasing in attendance at museums and theaters in direct response to the increase in their television arts viewing, the final result remains to be seen: quite likely, improvements in the quality of television screens and the advent of computerized information services might make stay-at-home museum visiting as well as attendance at lectures or films more desirable.

Nonetheless the basic finding of these new studies holds: the museum and its activities are located at the heart, not the fringe, of postindustrial society. We should not conveniently assume in a society moving toward information processing as its main occupation—that is, a service-oriented society requiring educated employees—that the museum will diminish rather than expand its role. Perhaps the persistence of the assumption that what we call "art" is a special preserve can be explained by the metaphorical appeal of the avant-garde, by the notion, stoked by dozens of films and hundreds of errant references in classrooms and historical texts, of the lone, heroic artist struggling against a hostile society. It is a metaphor based originally on the supposed rejection of the Impressionists in France during the 1860s. Completely aside from the historical inaccuracy—a number of Impressionists found collectors and critical recognition in their lifetimes, most of all Manet[7]—this hallowed tale has small relevance in the contemporary world, where literally millions of viewers, whetted by constant exposure to the lessons of art history (an unknown science in the last century), charge toward art museums and galleries with armed minds and tutored eyes. We must revise our figurative understanding of the avant-garde (and, by extension, art itself) as a boxer engaged in a slugging match under klieg lights with a small army of heavy-footed adversaries. Now he or she is a dancer engaged in a duet in which each partner leads and follows at once and where the final moves are unpredictable.

9
I.M. Pei and Partners.
East Building of the
National Gallery
of Art,
Washington, D.C.
Sketch of plan.

10
I.M. Pei and Partners.
East Building of the
National Gallery
of Art,
Washington, D.C.
Plan.

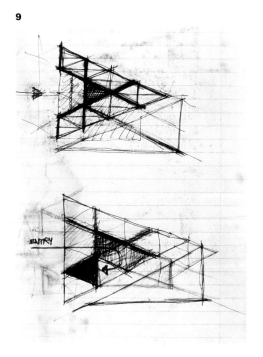

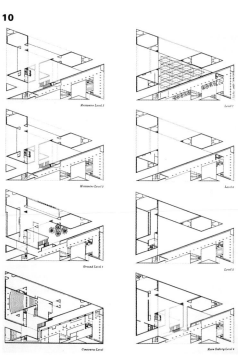

Institutions like museums, universities, and libraries have a different role to play in society, a noneconomic role.
—*Thomas Messer, quoted in* Museums for a New Century *(1984)*

Among the consequences of the quantitative increase in the museum audience is the more prominent position of the arts in the realm of public policy. The days are clearly over when private decisions could be made for private purposes, beyond public criticism. The Harris polls indicate that an overwhelming number of Americans (74 percent) believe the role of the arts in education should be increased through public funding. Equally dramatic percentages are committed to increasing federal and state support for artists, museums, and exhibitions; more than 70 percent are willing to pay an additional $5 per year in taxes to achieve this end.

But public support has inevitably invited public participation. By the end of the twentieth century, no American museum can expect to revise or reform either its program or its architecture without wide-open debate. In Europe, where sustained government support for the arts is an accepted fact, the same is true. Decisions to expand the Whitney and Guggenheim Museums in New York and to renovate the interiors of Pompidou Center and the Gare d'Orsay in Paris, as well as drastically to alter the entrance to the Louvre, have caused more heated commentary in the press and on the street than most issues of economic or military policy. In New York the architects at the eye of the storm—Michael Graves at the Whitney, Charles Gwathmey and Robert Siegel at the Guggenheim—were forced to present their cases over and over in press conferences and public hearings in 1986

and 1987. Paris in the mid-eighties equally excoriated Gae Aulenti, the revisionist architect for both Pompidou and d'Orsay, and the American architect I. M. Pei, whose glass pyramid now welcomes visitors to the center of the Louvre, although their cases were often argued by the French government, which bankrolled the projects. The protagonists here were, first, centrist president Valéry Giscard d'Estaing, followed by the ambitious socialist François Mitterand, who commissioned a wide range of extraordinary parks, office towers, and museums (collectively known as "the Grand Projects") between 1981 and 1988. Debates of equal ferocity attended the building and reformation of museums throughout Europe during this decade, particularly in Germany, where a surge of construction took place in the seventies and eighties, capped by the opening of the immense $250 million Museum Ludwig complex in Cologne, the interior volume of which (48,000 square feet) rivals the immense medieval cathedral towering above.

The grand irony lurking behind these debates and projects is clear. Compelled by ego and expectation to design in a high, uninhibited style, the architect of the museum time and again provoked public resistance. The passions aroused in the 1950s and 1960s by Frank Lloyd Wright and Marcel Breuer were minor compared to those seen several decades later when museums had become vital institutions for the entire population. Graves's oft-repeated contention that his decorative gray-pink granite "wing" for the Whitney gestures broadly to motifs prevalent in the surrounding neighborhood, as Breuer's massive geometrical forms intentionally did not, mattered not at all to the protestors, who included nearby residents and hundreds of architects. In a sense, Graves's sin, as well as the Whitney's, was that of realism. The museum desperately needed to expand, both to contain its huge audience and to display more than a fraction of its permanent collection; Graves's solution, surely rooted in the antimodernist rhetoric of the postmodern movement, was to achieve esthetic balance with Breuer's structure, one of the boldest forms devised in this century, linking the two by a cylinder bulging out from the south end of the older building. The Guggenheim's need to expand was even more urgent: its ratio of

attendance per square foot of space ranked second only to the National Gallery in Washington, D.C. The esthetic challenge presented by Wright's spiraling concrete structure was fully comparable to Breuer's. Gwathmey-Siegel rightly compared the compositional challenge to that of a collage or assemblage and in their first scheme, derided by critics, they presented a cantilevered addition covered with gray-green porcelain tile that gestured in its defiant geometry to Wright's defiant circle.

The ultimate solutions at both the Whitney and the Guggenheim represented scaled-down architectural ambition. In Paris neither Aulenti nor Pei were made to surrender or compromise, but the criticism that greeted them was based on a similar refusal to accept change, despite the extraordinary physical needs engendered by the very audience that resisted the solution. Aulenti's lavishly articulated galleries, which often obscured the architectonic grandeur of the old Gare d'Orsay, were as rational and predictable as

Graves's facade, Gwathmey-Siegel's geometrical verve, or the decision of any contemporary museum to expand beyond its Lilliputian proportions. She had intruded upon the Pompidou Center in precisely the same way the year before, in response to the same basic need: room-sized galleries for conventional exhibitions within an open, unconventional space that rivalled d'Orsay in sheer scale. And Pei's pristine pyramid, soundly belabored at first by the French for its refusal to echo the historical grandeur of the Louvre, gestured as forcefully to history as one could expect from a designer whose commitment to modernity and abstraction had been demonstrated for more than four decades. His archetypal pyramid gestured deep into the past, after all, back as far as ancient Egypt.

11

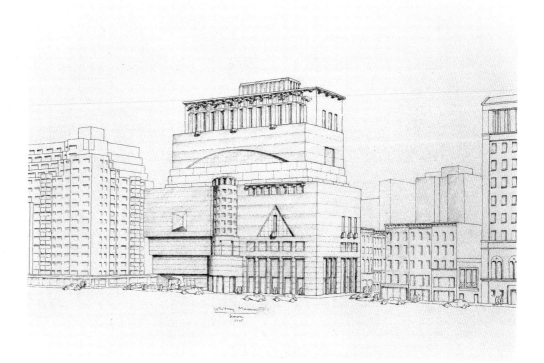

12

13

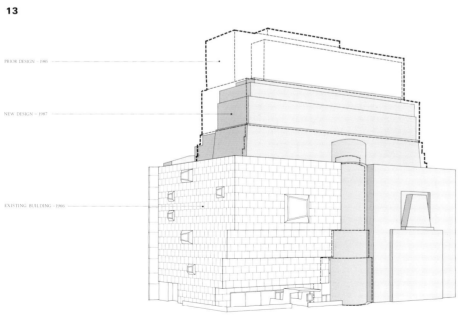

PRIOR DESIGN · 1985

NEW DESIGN · 1987

EXISTING BUILDING · 1966

11
*Michael Graves Architect.
Proposed addition to the Whitney Museum of American Art, New York. Drawing of first design, 1985.*

12
*Michael Graves Architect.
Proposed addition to the Whitney Museum of American Art, New York. Model of second design, 1987.*

13
*Michael Graves Architect.
Proposed addition to the Whitney Museum of American Art, New York. Comparison of designs from 1985 and 1987.*

But if the public outcry was in nearly all of these cases based on a refusal to face cultural reality, so too was the premise upon which the architects, for the most part, based their esthetic decisions. Contrary to the widely accepted belief, the museum is not a project that invites arbitrary stylistic invention; rather, it is a social and political organism: touch one pole, or corner, and you invite wrath as well as approval. By the end of the century, as political and technological evolution increasingly encourages widespread participation in public discussion, the presence of the public voice is certain to increase. If architecture—the most visible sign of the museum's presence—is the first target

of this change, surely programming or exhibition policy is next. The Harris surveys presented only the most obvious facts about museum attendance, rarely pausing to investigate the dark underside of its rosy numbers: why does half of the population fail to attend museums? British curator Roger Milles suggested at least one reason, arguing incisively that most museum exhibitions are assembled and installed for a "target" audience rather than the "real" audience, for colleagues and specialists rather than laymen.[8] The results include exhibitions that fail to present the social or historical context in which any art or craft occurs, and others that focus on subjects appropriate for small or specialized audiences rather than the large numbers now attending most public urban institutions. Based on studies in Europe and in the United States, Milles concludes that a tiny

14

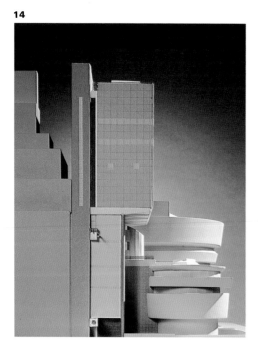

15

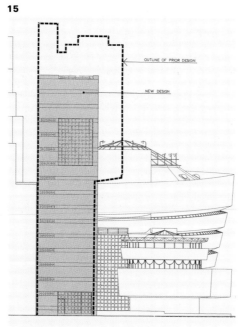

OUTLINE OF PRIOR DESIGN

NEW DESIGN

14
*Gwathmey Siegel
& Associates Architects.
Proposed addition to
the Guggenheim
Museum, New York.
Model of first design.*

15
*Gwathmey Siegel
& Associates Architects.
Proposed addition to
the Guggenheim
Museum, New York.
Comparison of designs
from 1985 and 1987.*

16
*Gwathmey Siegel
& Associates Architects.
Proposed addition to
the Guggenheim
Museum, New York.
Drawing of second
design.*

16

percentage of the real audience for the museum is made up of what he calls "serious buyers" motivated primarily by scholarly or curatorial concerns. The bulk of its visitors are there for social and broadly instructional purposes, or what might be called "education in the state of freedom"—education in a noncoercive atmosphere. Certainly the refusal of the museum profession to address its uniquely

educational role, exemplified by exhibitions presenting both art and science *sui generis*, without the intervention of textbook or teacher, is one of the major problems of this century. Its final resolution will surely modify, perhaps profoundly, the architecture of the museum.

17

In Which the Curtain Rises and the Plot Begins to Unfold

As the idea of his museum grew he came to realize the prejudice that had to be overcome before the new art, "nonobjective" as it was called, could be realized publicly.

Concerning this he said, "No such building as is now customary for museums could be appropriate for this one. I want a building to match the advanced painting I want to put in it. I believe you can do that building for me. I trust you."
—*Frank Lloyd Wright, letter to Harry Guggenheim (1952)*

Maybe I built it to rebel against skyscrapers and brownstones. I didn't try to fit the building to its neighbors because the neighboring buildings aren't any good.
—*Marcel Breuer, quoted in "The New Whitney," Newsweek (Oct. 3, 1966)*

Until the end of the Second World War, the architecture of the museum had been primarily shaped by preconceptions about its past. Frank Lloyd Wright was perfectly correct to identify his patron's wish to break with this pattern as exceptional. Nathaniel Burt is equally correct when he says the European program was defined by the royal and courtly collections at the heart of the Louvre, the Altes Museum, and beyond. Despite its didactic and democratic intentions, the American museum had consistently reflected these palatial origins, with their functional and programmatic as well as formal implications. The wholesale appropriation of classical conceits in the last century, particularly the use of the grand, arching entries, noble pillars, and long courtyard advocated by Durand, paradoxically linked the museum to the bank throughout the United States, where these forms were favored by the latter. Consistently the politics of both history and style led to a single result: the museum as treasure house. In virtually all of the debates that have occurred since then, even down to the choice of lighting systems, the museum-as-treasure house remains a fixed point in the polemic. The even, steady flow of artificial light is clearly preferable to those who view the contents of the museum as static, unquestioned treasures; the moving, changing quality of natural light is welcomed by those who see the museum as a more complex phenomenon, where temporal events and activities swirl around and beyond the viewing of treasures. The stubborn refusal

19

19
Frank Lloyd Wright.
Guggenheim Museum,
New York.

of those who commission or critique museum design to recognize the latter reality is difficult even for architects committed to the past for its own as value as well as its formal inspiration. Responding to the critics who pressed him about the ambition of his 97,920-square-foot addition to the Whitney's original 51,665-square-foot building, Michael Graves argued, in an open exchange at the Architectural League in New York in 1986, "I think this is a moment in history where we have to realize that we're not just building Kunsthalles or picture galleries. We're building institutions that have places for discussion, places for study, and a social climate as well as a climate in which to see painting and sculpture. I'm all in favor of that. I'm bowled over, quite frankly, that the building is described as too large."[9] The divide between the architecture of the palace and the architecture of what can now safely be called the anti-palace is deeper than normally acknowledged. The opposition engendered by Graves, Gwathmey, Pei, and Aulenti is simply the latest expression of a reflexive reaction that dates back through the first Whitney to Wright's Guggenheim and earlier to the opening of the old Louvre doors. What is implied by buildings that appear to depart from the realm of the muses—the vast steel-and-glass Pompidou Center in Paris by Richard Rogers and Renzo Piano; the deep, winding spiral of asymmetrical galleries at the Municipal Museum Abteiberg in Mönchengladbach, Germany, by Hans Hollein; the rough, bare factory walls of the Tempo-

rary Museum of Contemporary Art in Los Angeles by Frank Gehry—is an expansion of what might be called the esthetic intelligence to include vast areas of life once regarded as beyond artistic consideration, if not reform.

This book will chronicle that expansion, as well as a countercycle, particularly strong in the 1980s, that attempts to revive the palace and its cloistered ideals of reverence, meditation, and perfect maintenance of the king's treasures. As architecture, the new ambidextrous and androgynous museum, responding to divergent claims and needs, is virtually impossible to resolve in the manner of an office building or a hospital, where form and function are often easy to unite. In a classic tirade that anticipated the backlash against Michael Graves's Whitney, the Chicago architect Harry Weese once assailed "new museums" for their devotion to "contraptions" like escalators, ramps, and elevators ("vertical coffins," in Weese's words). "Bookstores and cafeterias are another source of sounds and smells," he said, that were conspicuously absent in the "pantheons, palaces, cathedrals, and castle keeps" of an earlier day.

But this is not an earlier day. The twentieth century is ending in the eddy of innumerable revolutions, technological as well as political, that have broadened beyond repair or return our access to knowledge and to the arts or "culture" in the

20

*Frank O. Gehry
& Associates.
"Temporary" Los Angeles
Museum of Contemporary
Art, Los Angeles.
Gallery installation.*

20

21

broad sense meant by Emerson. At the same time the available supply of unique totems sanctified by scholars and historians is dwindling fast, as one museum or public-spirited collector or donor after another claims them forever. In his intricate study of art collecting, Joseph Alsop contends that the "market" inevitably responds to totemic scarcity by certifying new or previously neglected artists and movements—by replacing "original" first-class art, in effect, with trumped-up second-rate substitutes.[10] This process, surely accelerating as the century ends, suggests that few museums can continue to identify themselves primarily as storehouses of sanctified masterpieces and wrap themselves in the royalist architecture that signifies this role.

The sizable sums now commanded by the once-scorned eighteenth-century *pompier* painters who toadied to the French aristocracy, not to say the nineteenth-century photographs derided by the poet Baudelaire as an affront to art, confirm Alsop's contention. Together they argue that the evolving museum must see itself as a medium of information and pleasure as well as a repository providing first-hand access to the sacred object—in brief, for a somewhat wider role, which might be termed "post-object" in the programmatic sense. To stand pat in the face of these circumstances—to continue to buy, collect, and enshrine whatever becomes available—condones nothing less than a form of materialist absurdity. In 1984, for instance, the American Association of Museums estimated that there were 1 billion "art" objects housed in American museums alone. The sprawling Smithsonian Institution in Washington, D.C., counted more than 137 million objects in its sprawling collection—paintings, posters, documents, toothbrushes—with a projected future growth rate of three percent each year (or 718,105 additional objects in 1989).

The Smithsonian is a paradigm of Alsop's thesis. Here the museum as the sacred realm of the masterpiece becomes instead a quantitative magnet for possessions of every kind with only secondary regard for intellectual or historical significance. What if a fraction of this incredible commitment were poured instead into the presentation of information about the world's authentic treasures, now easily recalled for our eyes and minds by electronic media or by holography, in media varying from the television set to the home computer (linked by modem to a fiber-optic delivery system) or to monitor terminals installed in the museum itself? Long ago the German critic Walter Benjamin prophesied that the mechanical reproduction of works of art through photography and film would diminish our insistence on confronting the "aura" of art only in its original state. Today the double coda of supply and demand—the one diminishing while the other rises—unexpectedly hastens the realization of his thesis. Now we have the means to "move" any treasure in a matter of seconds from the vault of the Louvre to a terminal in Columbus, Ohio, before a viewer conditioned by now to intuit the lost "aura" of a work of art in its duplicate state.

The architect who is aware of this post-contemporary condition—and of the museum's evolving role—is trapped in a fatal contradiction. He must somehow reconcile this truth with the demands of an institution generally committed to posing as the cathedral of the irreplaceable object. While the audience and the program of the museum move in one direction, the institution itself demands another. This honorable task is as difficult as the task of making high art itself. Here, the architect is doomed to exhilarating defeat.

Gae Aulenti.
Musée d'Orsay, Paris.
Gallery installation.

Chapter Two **P A R I S :   T H E   P A L A C E   O F   P L E A S U R E**

22
*Piano and Rogers/
Richard Rogers
Partnership.
Pompidou Center,
Paris.*

It is our belief that buildings should be able to change, not only in plan, but in section and elevation. A freedom which allows people freedom to do their own things, the order and scale and grain coming from a clear understanding and expression of the process of building . . . all within a clearly defined and rational framework. This framework must allow people to perform freely inside and out . . . becoming an expression of the architecture of the building—a grani Meccano set, rather than a traditional static transparent or white doll's house.
—Renzo Piano and Richard Rogers, quoted in Norman Foster, Richard Rogers, James Stirling *(1971)*

The first sighting of the Pompidou Center in the late l970s may rank with the moon landing among the epiphanies of our time. Journalists, architects, and schoolchildren called the structure everything from "an architectural King Kong" and "an exploded tinkertoy" to "a stranded space ship." Most critics found the Pompidou intolerable, or at least impossible to accept as a museum in the conventional sense. Bereft of traditional ornamentation, this steel-and-glass skeleton was built between 1975 and 1978 on a drab 5-acre lot situated in what was known, ironically, as the *Plateau Beaubourg*, or "pretty town." Its brash young architects, Renzo Piano of Italy and Richard Rogers of England, removed the servicing ducts, pipes, and electrical boxes from the core of the building, painted them in bold primary colors, and hung them on the exterior of the skeleton. Colors were keyed to usage: red represented movement (staircases, escalators); orange covered all ducts that housed electrical circuitry; blue stood for ventilation; green indicated water. Modern form had at last found a rainbow, in effect, to depict function.

Before the rainbow, out on the huge plaza that surrounds Pompidou, visitors encounter hundreds of fellow citizens strolling, chatting, or watching the dozens of wandering dancers and musicians who fill the air with the music of drums, banjos, trumpets, and more. They are there from morning until late in the evening, never allowing the muses a moment for meditation or retreat.

The interior of the Piano-Rogers structure distressed its critics even more. Upon entering, visitors found themselves not in a foyer leading logically to a series of rooms arranged around a formal and predictable axis, but rather inside a giant, five-story atrium filled with overpowering works of sculpture as well as platoons of people—an atrium that made the rest of the enormous building (544.5 feet long, 196 feet wide, 137.75 feet high) seem no more than a shell. Pompidou Center housed the Musée National d'Art Moderne on the top three floors, each floor as open, column-free, and inviting of the antic expansionism of contemporary art as the atrium below. But the building contained not only art. An innovative, open-stack library, the Bibliothèque Publique d'Information, replete with films and videocassettes and accessible seven days a week was installed on the second, third, and fourth levels. The basement level featured the Centre de Création Industrielle, devoted to displays of architecture and design. Cinemas, restaurants, and cafes appeared throughout the building, and nearby in an adjacent wing, a center for new music opened, directed by the famous conductor Pierre Boulez.

In no sense was a visit to the Pompidou Center comparable to attendance of any conventional museum, least of all in the country of its birth, where museums were noted for their short hours and sanctimonious solitude. Instead, this startling

23

24

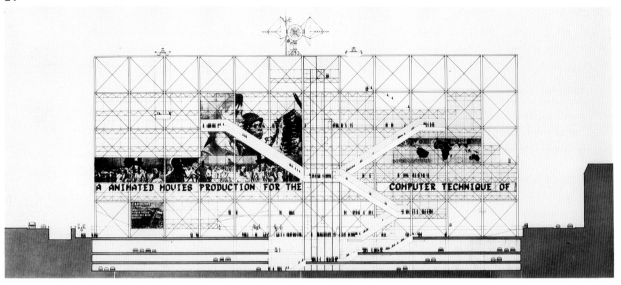

24
*Piano and Rogers/
Richard Rogers
Partnership.
Pompidou Center,
Paris.
Drawing of lateral
facade.*

25
*Piano and Rogers/
Richard Rogers
Partnership.
Pompidou Center,
Paris.
Gallery installation.*

new museum seemed akin to the theater or an open-air concert. Every day thousands of visitors would ride the glass-walled escalators on the exterior merely to gaze at the unparalleled views of the Paris cityscape they afforded, and at the Rabelaisian hordes on the plaza below.

The abiding question is not only how Pompidou came to be, but why, particularly in a city and nation not noted for its willingness to defy tradition. One of the jurors who decided in the end to commission this extraordinary work, Philip Johnson, recalls that the mood in Paris in the early 1970s was truculent. Once the recognized art capital of the world, over the previous few decades Paris had seen its mantle seized by New York. Shortly after he arrived, Johnson was approached by the president of France, Georges Pompidou, an active collector of modern art, and grilled for information about exhibitions and trends in New York—a singular concession at a moment when most French citizens were content to rest on their laurels. Indeed, it was Pompidou's steadfast support for the new museum that kept it on track in later years, despite heated internal disputes between a miscellany of curators and administrators, as well as opposition from the general press and more specialized critics. The final decision by the jury in favor of the unknown Piano-Rogers team of course provoked immediate opposition from the public and resentment within the cumbersome official bureaucracy. But alone among the 681 entries, only Piano and Rogers offered a convincing alternative to the conventional museum. No one could doubt that this structure, when completed, would command the attention of the world and lay to rest any doubts about Paris's esthetic vitality or daring. In its plasticity, flexibility, and in its saucy refusal to proclaim a traditional iconic identity, the scheme also of-

fered the institution a certain internal political salvation, allowing its sparring curatorial departments to articulate their own spaces in response to their particular needs.

In an important sense, then, both the Pompidou Center and the Louvre were products of their times, as well as the results of intense debate and speculation. But here the analogy ends. The Louvre was a ceremonial structure originally dedicated to ends other than art, as were the legions of temples, tombs, villas, and cathedrals later converted into museums. As Carol Duncan and Alan Wallach have noted, its primary function was ideological in the deepest national sense:[11] even the revolutionaries expected the Louvre to impress upon the public the grandeur of the state and to reflect its official beliefs. Inside, except on the days when artists and their pupils copied the masters, the atmosphere in the palace was sober if not sacrosanct. But Richard Rogers thought of the Pompidou Center from the start as a contradiction of these attitudes. On his earliest drawings and plans he called it "a building for culture, information, and entertainment."[12] The Piano-Rogers proposal was, as we can see, iconoclastic in the lowest as well as the highest sense. By keeping this transparent, flexible, and welcoming space open late into the evening and filling it with life, food, and drink, as well as books, art, film, and lectures, the museum's leaders—among them the formidable and accomplished Pontus Hulten, lured from the Moderna Museet in Stockholm—were indeed providing "entertainment" that matched anything currently available in Paris or perhaps in the world.

From its opening week in 1977, the Pompidou Center proved to be an overwhelming popular success, averaging twenty thousand daily visitors during the week and more than double that number on Sundays—figures exceeding original

projections by four to five times. But its fate on a higher critical level is a far more complex matter. Clearly the stylistic influence of the Piano-Rogers building was at first negligible, with a few exceptions such as Norman Foster's Sainsbury Centre in Norwich, England, or a number of museums dedicated to the industrial or scientific arts like the National Air and Space Museum in Washington, D.C., by Hellmuth, Obata, and Kassabaum. The predominant obsession in the post-Pompidou years remained traditional: Schinkel, not Mies, and definitely not Piano and Rogers, was the guiding spirit of museum architecture, at least on the surface.

Yet as a programmatic model the Pompidou Center was decisively effective. The hybrid building type that critics began in the late 1980s to call the "last generation" museum in fact defines itself by a programmatic complexity (with restaurants, libraries, theaters, shops) that clearly imitates the Pompidou program. Often, now, rooms or auditoriums have to be used for a wide variety of purposes: walls must be easily moved or lowered, skylights boarded up, partitions added or removed. This situation further dictates a spatial organization first introduced in large scale at Pompidou. The vast welcoming atrium, hall, or rotunda from which the entire organization of the building can be instantly perceived is required not only by the increased number of visitors but by the need to render complex options clearly visible. I. M. Pei's East Building of the National Gallery in Washington, D.C., Louis Kahn's Yale Center for British Art, and James Stirling's Staatsgalerie in Stuttgart are all examples of this configuration, unnecessary in the days of the converted palace or shrine when only the leisured pilgrim in search of the masterpiece was anticipated.

The Pompidou Center became a turning point in the design of museums by stating the case for the desanctification of art—for the museum as a container of "culture" in the broad, vulgar sense—with such force that it could not be ignored. After Pompidou, both the museum community and its architects were either forced to reject this standard or accept its implications. What Piano and Rogers had wrought could not be ignored. In this sense, Georges Pompidou's legacy was exactly as he'd wished: through architecture if not art Paris was restored to center stage. Both of his immediate successors to the presidency, Valéry Giscard d'Estaing and François Mitterand, emboldened by his example, continued to build, convert, and restore museums in a grand style. In 1973 Giscard, decidedly antimodern in his own collecting taste, decided to convert the huge old railway station on the Left Bank of the Seine, the Gare d'Orsay, into a museum devoted entirely to nineteenth-century art, filling it with both well-known and obscure treasures raided from the Louvre and other institutions. A.C.T. Architecture won a competition between six French firms to renovate the exterior and interior of the 350,000-square-foot, barrel-vaulted iron structure erected in 1898 by Victor Laloux to salute the glories of the train specifically and the Industrial Revolution in general. But A.C.T.'s efforts within the interior failed ignominiously. This debacle prompted a second competition, won in 1980 by the ambitious Italian designer Gae Aulenti, who ultimately decided to contradict Laloux, the train, and the Industrial Revolution entirely, if not the aristocratic Giscard.

Although Giscard's conversion of d'Orsay was an expensive decision, costing more than $250 million, his building program was timid compared to that of Mitterand, his socialist successor. In 1982 Mitterand launched a series of "Grand Projects" that ultimately required nearly $3 billion. While they included opera houses, office buildings, and an innovative urban "park" designed by a young Swiss architect named Bernard Tschumi, which included galleries and spaces for cultural activities, it was the Louvre again that stood at the center of events. In 1983 Mitterand selected I. M. Pei, an American architect born in China, to revamp and reform this holy ground. When Pei revealed plans and models in the manner of the upstart Pompidou for an underground network of conference rooms, cafeterias, workshops, and parking spaces, topped by a steel-and-glass pyramid, the public, in France and around the world, was initially enraged. Angry editorials and heated denunciations followed. If Paris had first spawned the museum, it also seemed—two hundred years later—to be redefining its architectural and ideological parameters.

26

The Musée d'Orsay, emerging from the ghost of the old Gare d'Orsay, exemplified this challenge. Giscard had originally intended that the museum cover virtually the entire sweep of the nineteenth century; several French leaders had preferred that it close at 1860 with the grand return of Louis-Napoleon and imperial ambition. When elected, Mitterand and his colleague Madeline Rebérioux, a Marxist art historian, both insisted that the collection begin with 1848, the beginning of the Second Republic and the legacy of the Revolution, closing in 1914 with the outbreak of the First World War. But it is clear that neither Mitterand nor Rebérioux, later appointed vice president of d'Orsay, were able completely to control the interior design or the initial installation of the collection. As the radical character of the Pompidou Center defied the conservative government that built it, so too did the intransigent nostalgia of Aulenti's Musée d'Orsay mock its socialist heirs.

When the vast interior of the old station was turned over to Gae Aulenti, the flamboyant die was cast. Although she often talked about the necessity of subordinating architecture to art, Aulenti was far too inventive to allow either side of the equation to upstage her. She installed two long, narrow, 20-foot stone structures knifing through the center of the station's immense, 450-foot-long, glass-roofed central hall. They turned this once epic and transparent space into a roseate promenade, recalling the ceremonial entrances

27

Gae Aulenti.
Musée d'Orsay, Paris.
Section drawing of
interior renovation.

28

Gae Aulenti.
Musée d'Orsay, Paris.
View of central corridor.

29

Gae Aulenti.
Musée d'Orsay, Paris.
Gallery installation.

27

28

29

to pyramids and the naves of immense cathedrals. The terraces and mock roofs along the promenade were filled with nineteenth-century sculpture of every conceivable style and derivation. An equally diverse collection of paintings, drawings, and photographs filled a series of conventional gallery spaces defined by rough stone walls. At the far end of the old station, Aulenti trumped her procession with two mighty obelisks directing the visitor to galleries containing more paintings and decorative arts. All of the galleries and corridors were marked by gray- and rose-colored partitions, pedestals, and platforms. Hundreds of paintings, objects, and photographs were crowded into this busy yet stately space, perfectly fulfilling the claims of the museum's directors that the new museum would "show everything," and end as nothing less than "a museum of civilization."

But in fact the Musée d'Orsay's reading of civilization's history, like its saccharine interior, promulgated a strong political point of view. Just as Aulenti had eclipsed the magnificent late-industrial architecture of Victor Laloux, so had the curators established a neo-conservative interpretation of nineteenth-century art. The priceless Jeu de Paume collection of Impressionist paintings—produced by the artists who defied the state salons in the middle of the last century and who launched the very idea of an "avant-garde" beholden to no external power—was tucked away for the most part in the museum's garret, on the top floor. Down below, engaging the large and curious crowds lured in the opening months of 1986 and into 1987, were the once-despised *pompier* painters, most of whom performed obsequious service to the state in the eighteenth century by rendering apocryphal portraits of kings, queens, generals, and wealthy aristocrats. That they were occasionally juxtaposed with rebellious colleagues—on the bottom floor, the courtly Jean-Auguste-Dominique Ingres, Alexandre Cabanel, and Thomas Couture leered across the promenade at Honoré Daumier, Jean François Millet, and Gustave Courbet—further infuriated those who dispute what was clearly a neo-conservative interpretation of the nineteenth century.[13] Up above, Manet's *Olympia*, Puvis de Chavannes's *Women by the Seashore*, and Cormon's *Cain*, straining for a photographic immediacy of representation and a bold abstract sense of composition, were clearly shipwrecked within Aulenti's lavish, classically articulated galleries.

I am keenly aware of
the many banalities
built in its name over
the years. Nevertheless,
I believe in the continu-
ity of this tradition [the
modern movement] for
it is by no means a relic
of the past.
—I.M. Pei, acceptance
speech for the Pritzker
Prize for Architecture
(1983)

I. M. Pei represented the polar extreme
from Aulenti, as did the Louvre project itself. Whereas d'Orsay attempts to redefine
and restore the values of the past by en-
shrining the *pompiers* and restoring grandeur in the galleries, the Louvre reaches
out to the present, practically as well as
symbolically. Both Mitterand and the administrators of the Louvre recognized as
early as 1981 that the museum was in a
shocking state of disrepair; furthermore,
the basement areas devoted to storage and
restoration of the immense, deteriorating
collection were disastrously limited in
terms of space. Finally, the long "occupation" of the grand northern wing of the
Louvre by the Ministry of Finance was
clearly inappropriate. In 1982 Mitterand
appointed a committee of advisors headed
by Emile J. Biasini to plan the final resolution. One year later, based on Biasini's
recommendations and his own strong con-
viction, Mitterand appointed Pei to design
a new and aggressively "open" entrance
space for the beleaguered Louvre, as well
as an underground network of service
spaces. In 1984, in the face of protests,
Pei's plan was unveiled and ultimately
approved. With the aid of Mitterand's
unwavering support and enthusiasm, the
work was completed in 1988 in time for the
bicentennial of the Revolution that had in
fact fathered the museum.

Pei's choice of the pyramid for the entrance to the Louvre provided the institution with a symbolic center for the first
time. At first derided for its sterility, the
form of the pyramid, ubiquitous in both

Eastern and Western cultures, creates a
powerful mediation point between past and
present. Flanked by the northern wing,
Pei's glass-and-steel pyramid rises 70 feet
on a 115-foot-wide base from the center
of a 22-acre site, clearly separating the
Louvre from itself. Here the visitor is ori-
ented immediately by means of wall texts,
video monitors, and staff to the entire
range of choices available in the museum.
Below there is a vast subterranean world of
conference rooms and sales rooms, storage
areas and restoration workshops—so vast,
in fact, that it almost doubles the Louvre's
internal space, to 1,398,800 square feet.

Certainly the clean, lithe neutrality of
Pei's solution enabled him to avoid the fate
that befell Gian Lorenzo Bernini, the Italian baroque master imported by Louis XV
in the seventeenth century to provide a
grand new entrance for the east facade but
dismissed within two years for both esthetic and political reasons. When debate
in the press was heating up in 1984, Pei
received crucial support from the curatorial staff of the Louvre, which voted
overwhelmingly—and publicly—to support
him. Surely the curators were motivated,
as the critics were not, by the Louvre's
need to accommodate a complex series of
demands foisted upon it by the viewing
public.

The Pei proposal responded, as Aulenti's interior at d'Orsay did not, to the
necessity for complex decision making in
the last-generation museum. Aulenti in-

stead deluged the viewer with ideological commentary masked as the decorative enhancement of "art." When questioned about her earlier reinstallation of gallery spaces at Pompidou in 1985, which offered equally intrusive interior details, she replied, "For me, in general, architecture is durable art and science. . . . The Pompidou Center was born with a program highly linked to mobility and at a period when the ideology of flexibility was in the culture. When the curators asked me to work with them, they indicated . . . that the mobility of the collection had to express itself in a new way. . . ."[14] The director of the Musée National d'Art Moderne at the time, Dominique Bozo, Hulten's successor, went further, suggesting that the original Piano-Rogers plan offered too few traditional gallery spaces and in fact too much flexibility. "A museum," he argued, "is above all a collection and a space for presentation."

30

30
I.M. Pei and Partners.
Addition to the Louvre,
Paris.
Model of site.

31
I.M. Pei and Partners.
Addition to the Louvre,
Paris.

31

49

32
I.M. Pei and Partners.
Addition to the Louvre,
Paris.
Site plan.

33
I.M. Pei and Partners.
Addition to the Louvre,
Paris.
Entrance.

34
I.M. Pei and Partners.
Addition to the Louvre,
Paris.
Model with view of
interior.

32

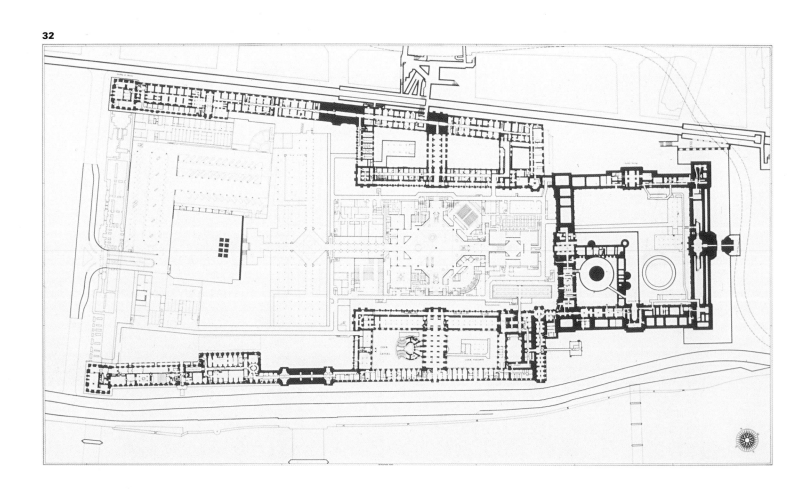

33

34

Certainly the Bozo-Aulenti position appeared effectively to counter the radical proposition offered in 1978 by the Pompidou Center. A return to the palace of "rooms" (as opposed to "spaces") was often evident in the mid-eighties, in Paris and elsewhere around the world. During these years the Musée d'Orsay loomed large in the minds of critics and curators. The elegant renovation and conversion of the blond-stone Hôtel Salé into the Picasso Museum in 1985 was typical. Raymond Simounet emerged triumphant from the competition for this task essentially by proposing minimal changes to the interior of a home reared in 1656 for an elderly nouveau riche merchant. This palatial structure was deemed a perfect home for the personal collection of one of the century's most mercurial and challenging painters (a collection that fell into public hands, managed by the Ministry of Culture, in lieu of estate taxes). The grand staircase and vestibule, redolent of an ear-lier era, are virtually unchanged. The old ceilings on the first floor are completely restored, as is the stone ornamentation in the salon and the huge hoop-shaped courtyard. Only above, in the semipublic offices, drawing center, and documentation center did the architect gut and reform the interior spaces. Deftly turned, the Hôtel Salé is nonetheless a contradictory space in which to view the changing styles of Picasso's own work and that of the artists he admired, befriended, and collected, dating back to 1901 and including such pure and primitive moderns as Cézanne, Degas, Matisse, Rousseau, Derain, and Balthus. Closed in its traditional references, confining in its predominantly bourgeois layout, the old Hôtel contradicts the premise and spirit of the work it displays.

35

35

*Main facade of
Picasso Museum,
Paris,
renovated by Roland
Simounet.*

36
Roland Simounet.
Picasso Museum,
Paris.
Gallery installation.

36

The divide in Paris between Pompidou and the reborn Louvre on the one hand and the d'Orsay–Hôtel Salé on the other is instructive, as are their connections. The former two openly proclaim their commitment to contemporary complexity of usage while the latter attempt to reform what Aulenti called "the ideology of flexibility." Both d'Orsay and the Picasso Museum confront the viewer with a barrage of historical references. That they often contradict the meaning of the collection or the building itself (in the case of d'Orsay) is clearly less important to their curators and architects than the symbolic commitment to the grand palatial tradition of "art" itself. Aulenti never pretended that her fanciful collage of Egyptian and neoclassical motifs alludes precisely to the cultural conditions of the nineteenth century. Obviously she intended to evoke the aura that enfolded the entire century, although the building is interspersed with ostentatious references to the present, to the "double coding" inherent in all renovation (wire mesh in partitions and railings; holes drilled into the stone walls to serve as picture hangers). In the name of restoring context, Aulenti and her colleagues had substituted idiosyncratic reading of history.

It could be argued that Pompidou itself represented a "reading" rather than a neutral container. In an early review of the structure, Hilton Kramer at once praised the "King Kong" of architecture for fitting surprisingly well into its surroundings while protesting that its "neutrality" and "flexibility" were delusions revoked by a radical, multivalent presence that defies traditional methods of isolating "high" art. But surely Piano and Rogers were correct when they later argued that "flexibility" is a chameleonic virtue: the wide-open halls of their building lay in wait to be defined by their users no matter what their programmatic preferences. When Bozo decided that access to the collection had to be simplified, he did not have to hesitate: visitors now enter the fourth exhibition level directly from the sculpture garden. When he decided to restore what he considered to be the imbalance between lectures, films, performances, and the viewing of "art," he simply transformed, with Aulenti, an open temporary exhibition space into a series of simple, clean-limbed rooms with traditional passageways and alcoves.

Rather than abandoning the palace of pleasure, in other words, Bozo and Aulenti in fact paid it the ultimate compliment by proving that it was capable of reverse transformation. Even those critics who complained about the deterioration of the plant betrayed a similar irony. The trampling feet that soon wore down the fiberglass carpets installed by Aulenti to protect the floors; the congestion brought about by tens of thousands of daily museum goers, only a quarter of whom came to visit art exhibitions; the insufficient number of gallery walls large enough to accommodate the rapidly expanding collection and the public appetite—all these factors con-

37

Roland Simounet.
Picasso Museum,
Paris.
Renovation of interior
stairway.

38

Roland Simounet.
Picasso Museum,
Paris.
Gallery installation.

38

39

firmed the building's popularity as well as its utility. By seducing its audience and reforming in response to changing curatorial patterns, Piano and Rogers's radical modernity revealed its rationale. Unlike Picasso and d'Orsay, the Pompidou Center did not double-code itself. The interior plan assumed that contemporary cultural patterns could not be imposed upon the structure or the viewer as content. To this day, Pompidou simply attempts to envelop, not define, a future that will inevitably shift (as it did under Bozo and Aulenti) and then shift again, as it did in 1987 when Hulten returned as a consultant, following Bozo's resignation, bringing a renewed emphasis on "contemporary" forms of art.

From the point of view of its critics, the Pompidou Center had become a palace of pleasure masquerading as a cultural center. In the eyes and minds of its defenders, Pompidou was destined, along with recent museums everywhere, to question the traditional limitations on both museum programs and audiences. In a century when the engines of both education and the postindustrial economy are beginning to liberate the middle class from the suffocating insularity of low-paid, unskilled labor, the arts have become common property. The enduring legacy of the Pompidou Center is this: that it signified this fact before it became common knowledge.

39
Piano and Rogers/
Richard Rogers
Partnership.
Pompidou Center,
Paris.

Chapter Three   THE MUSEUM AFTER POMPIDOU:
IMPERIALISM/
POPULISM/
CONTRADICTION

40
Richard Meier &
Partners.
High Museum of Art,
Atlanta, Georgia.
Main entrance.

Whatever we see could be other than it is.
—Ludwig Wittgenstein, The Limits of My Language Are the Limits of My World *(1921)*

The circulation, lighting, installation, and spatial qualities of the design are intended to encourage people to experience the art of architecture as well as the art displayed.
—Richard Meier, statement for the High Museum, Atlanta (1983)

Architecture as a pure art—equivalent to sculpture and painting, art as practiced by Michelangelo, Velázquez, Picasso . . . to us the art of architecture is a matter of greater importance than any activity known to mankind. Our art includes all others. . . . Our art may create forms for the next thousand years.
—Philip Johnson, address to the American Institute of Architects (1987)

Edmund Burke once described Marie Antoinette's gait as airborne; as she entered a drawing room her feet appeared to rise ever so slightly, a critical matter of inches. The High Museum of Art in Atlanta by Richard Meier presents a similar illusion. Although it is rooted firmly in the ground, the High appears elevated on approach, particularly when sunlight bounces off its white porcelain panels. At those moments the High is reminiscent of Karl Friedrich Schinkel's magnificent Altes Museum in East Berlin and Mies van der Rohe's pristine new National Gallery in West Berlin, both of which are dramatically perched on podia that elevate them symbolically above the world, as if art were on a pedestal. Indeed Mies's platform gestures intentionally across the city to Schinkel, his neoclassical master.

The High rises on a gentle slope in a park on Peachtree Street in the middle of Atlanta, but its podium is implicit in its every architectural detail. Perhaps more completely and certainly more skillfully than anywhere else, the High embodies the antithesis of the Pompidou Center. In company with many of the museums constructed in the United States and abroad during the halcyon years that directly preceded and followed the creation of the gentle monster in Beaubourg, the High means to set both itself and the art it displays apart from the life of the street. In writing about the Atlanta building, Meier explicitly confirms this point when he proclaims his intention to unveil the "art of architecture" as well as "the art itself." In this

41

42
Richard Meier &
Partners.
High Museum of Art,
Atlanta, Georgia.
Interior.

43
Richard Meier &
Partners.
High Museum of Art,
Atlanta, Georgia.
Interior.

statement, Meier summarizes a position held by many of his colleagues, particularly in the United States, during the years when architecture surrendered not only its high modern commitment to function and utility as primary goals but its historic claim—in the elaboration of grand, ceremonial buildings—to represent a higher social will. Now, perhaps for the first time in history, the architect begins to think of himself, of his own esthetic code, as a proper and almost an ordained goal. If Pompidou claimed for the museum a new, intensely public function, the meticulous High claimed it for a singularly private purpose.

Despite its beauty, the High cannot be considered in any sense a hospitable container for works of art, nor does it convey, as Meier also claimed in his statement, "a sense of the museum as a contemplative place." The High is the

legacy of the gilt-edged 1970s and 1980s, when fashion, commerce, and circumstance combined to create a distinctly estheticized cultural imperialism. The High is its own self-sufficient, self-ennobling end. Appropriately, its magnificent 67-foot-high atrium contains no art whatsoever. In Atlanta and elsewhere, the container became contained.

But the regal bearing of the High and its colleagues was hardly ordained from above in the manner of Louis xv opening the Luxembourg Gallery. No, this imperial hauteur responded precisely to the demands and needs of those who funded, managed, and attended the new building. Meier gave to Atlanta what it asked for and needed. While the High had been founded by Mr. and Mrs. Joseph High in 1926, three years before the Museum of Modern Art in New York opened, it had grown slowly. When Meier was commissioned in 1982, the institution owned few first-rate works of art from any period, past or present. Local collectors had been conspicuously reticent about leaving their caches to a museum that had occupied indifferent quarters from the beginning. Not until more than a hundred of Atlanta's cultural leaders died in a plane crash near Paris in 1962 did the city wake with a start, shocked by the catastrophe, and attempt to revive its esthetic life.

42

43

One year later a professional museum director, Gudmund Vigtel, was hired to lead the High, and not long after it was given space in the new, multipurpose Memorial Arts Building, raised in honor of the lost Atlantans. Though he had no endowment funds to purchase art until 1981 Vigtel began to beg, borrow, and scratch out the funds for occasional purchases during these years. The prospect of a new self-contained High was finally envisioned when Robert Woodruff, the president of Coca-Cola, offered a $7.5 million gift, which was later supplemented by business and political leaders who correctly sensed that the city, struggling to shed its Deep South legacy, needed a new symbol.

New York's Richard Meier, selected after an intensive search, was the perfect answer. Unlike the little-known Renzo Piano and Richard Rogers in Paris, and despite his youth, Meier carried an impeccable pedigree. He was noted for his elegant, pure white houses and public buildings, for his pristine geometry, for his ability to charm critics and collectors. Where Georges Pompidou and staid Paris sought provocation, young Atlanta wanted certification and haute monde approval. With every square inch, Meier's High proclaims its allegiance to the fine arts, not its separation. The impact of the long rising ramp leading to its door from the street level, of the gridded porcelain-steel plates that form its white-on-white skin, of the textbook "modern" cubes, boxes, and circles positioned at every corner, all this is unmistakable. The High certifies both itself and its city as serious converts to an esthetic religion.

But once inside the spectacular atrium capped by a fan-shaped skylight, we see only glistening white walls empty of art. The ostensible reason for this void is the destructive power of sunlight, which slowly erodes patinas of every variety. But the deeper reason is surely the decision to cede the drama of the High to its powerful architecture, not its modest collection. More than one dyspeptic critic has pointed out that less than half the High's space (a mere 46,000 square feet) is devoted to the display of art. From the atrium the visitor can barely detect the presence of upper-level galleries reached by a series of curved, narrow ramps reminiscent of Frank Lloyd Wright's broader spirals at the Solomon R. Guggenheim Museum in New York. On each floor, however, these galleries call immediate attention to themselves. Many are intimate in size, set off from the main circulation path, and pierced with windows that open out into the building, inviting the viewer to look away from the walls and toward the breathtaking formal vistas beyond—that is, into more architecture, not art. The galleries wind in and out of each other, with the palette of the interiors constantly changing from green-gray to lavender-gray to blue-gray. Columns fill the narrow void between these galleries as does an occasional chair or table, again designed by the architect, who also supervised the installation of the exhibitions at the public opening of the High in October 1983.

44
*Richard Meier &
Partners.
High Museum of Art,
Atlanta, Georgia.
Atrium.*

Like the Venus of Velázquez before her mirror, the High primps and poses on every floor, as do its visitors, who are clearly delighted to see themselves and each other framed in the reflective power of the High's facade. Meier's High certainly attains the ideal of "architecture as a pure art" voiced by Philip Johnson in his emotional address to the American Institute of Architects in 1987. Beyond that it exemplifies the picturesque ideal first forcefully defined by Robert Venturi in his seminal text *Complexity and Contradiction in Architecture* (1966). At the High, and among dozens of other new museums brought to life by hordes of freshly gentrified art lovers for whom no city, state, national, or corporate budget seemed large enough to please, the appearance (as opposed to the use) of the museum was proclaimed all-important. From the porcelain plates on the exterior of the High to the Lockheed Starfighter suspended by Frank Gehry from the side of the Aerospace Museum in Los Angeles, from the blue, red, yellow, and green handrails on James Stirling's Staatsgalerie in Stuttgart to the Franco-Spanish terra-cotta roofs on Philip Johnson and John Burgee's Center for the Fine Arts in Miami, the visual impact of new museums became paramount. Venturi had gently documented for his readers the abundant evidence that architects had often denied in their facades the uses of their interiors; "form" does not automatically follow "function," he pointed out, even in the mind of Louis Sullivan, who first uttered that phrase, and particularly in the

architecture of the seventeenth-century Italian baroque period. But many students, clients, and architects have construed this historical reminder as license to paint, primp, and thunder.

The "art" of architecture, often interpreted as visual aggression, quickly gained prominence. An exhibition curated by Helen Searing at the Whitney Museum of American Art in 1982 entitled *New American Art Museums* summarized the new orthodoxy. Presenting models, plans, and drawings, Searing focused on seven structures including the High, of course, Henry Cobb's Portland Museum in Maine, the Virginia Museum of Fine Arts addition by Hardy, Holzman, Pfeifer, Cesar Pelli's renovated Museum of Modern Art in New York, and even Edward Larrabee Barnes's Dallas Museum of Art. Searing wrapped her offerings in a conceptual context that stressed iconic presence rather than usage. The "self-effacing warehouse" is no longer a relevant model, she announced; the Miesian ideal of open, flowing space has been discarded for the symmetrical organization of rooms around a central courtyard, much in the manner proposed by French theorist J.N.L. Durand in 1805. But Searing, to her credit, also saw that the critical transition between the "warehouse" allegedly championed by the early modernists and the Venusian museum was found in the work of Louis Kahn, whose Yale Center for British Art (1977) has skillfully blended archetypal and contemporary elements. Kahn's travertine-and-oak interior, for instance, was balanced by a decidedly humble glass-and-stainless steel exterior that mirrored its neighbors, including the Yale Art Gallery (1972), one of Kahn's early masterpieces, and a building that glorifies function by transforming

its "servant" electrical and mechanical ducts into a lyrically gridded ceiling. It is no accident that virtually all the architects discussed in this chapter—despite their clear philosophical and stylistic differences—proclaimed fealty to Kahn, whose work stands in the vital center of the modern-postmodern battlefield.

Kahn's innovative attempt to blend a multiplicity of commercial needs into the sacrosanct cultural envelope of the Center for British Art was particularly notable. Fusing ground-floor shops with classrooms, libraries, and exhibition galleries, Kahn linked them all to a light-filled central court that rises through the entire height of the Center, permitting instant visual contact with its form and its programmatic richness, which encompassed research and teaching as well as exhibitions—and commerce. Meier's High is in fact more closely related to the complexity of this program than to Wright's Guggenheim, with which it is usually compared. Both at Yale and in Atlanta the architects faced a more substantial set of functional and political issues than did Wright, who was simply asked to provide soaring exhibition space for a single, uncompromising client. Meier, on the other hand, was implicitly challenged by the fund-raising slogan that preceded him: *Let's Give Atlanta the Museum It Deserves*.

As the shrine of an elit-
ist religion and at the
same time a utilitarian
instrument for demo-
cratic education, the
museum may be said to
have suffered from
schizophrenia from the
start. . . . The mu-
seum has always occu-
pied an ambiguous
position in radical
thought and action.
—Linda Nochlin, "Mu-
seums and Radicals"
(1971)

Unlike their European and Japanese coun-
terparts, who enjoyed the luxury of public
funding, virtually every American museum
reared during this period was subtly
molded by the demands of promotion and
publicity. Although Philip Johnson and
John Burgee were roundly criticized for
their decision to endow the Center for the
Fine Arts in Miami with a contrived over-
lay of historicist mission-style charm, their
choice was obviously prompted by a set of
commercial demands alien to classical theory. The museum had no collection at all,
downstaging even the High. The only way
to establish itself, therefore, was as a picturesque attraction amid a rapidly changing downtown that had been invaded by
brutal skyscraping office towers. Museum
officials often privately admitted that they
hoped to survive in the early years primarily as an air-conditioned mecca in the
midst of small shops, stores, and gargan-
tuan highrises. To this day this cream-
colored Spanish-American hybrid,
mounted on a 14-foot high podium that out-
does even Schinkel and Mies, stands as a
visual magnet, fulfilling a "need" hardly
anticipated by Palladio or Schinkel. Even
the uproar occasioned among local architects when the Johnson-Burgee plans were
first unveiled served a key purpose inherent in the stylistic change we are studying.

As the cosmeticized museum has
edged into the center of society, it has
joined with corporations and entrepreneurs
in competition for political and economic
power. The aggressive visual strategy
of the *esthétique royale* is more closely

aligned with political and programmatic complexity than we have acknowledged. Often august if not revivalist in appearance, the post-Pompidou museum betrays a contradictory populism. The buildings created by Barnes in Dallas and Arata Isozaki in Los Angeles were both generated by broad-based if occasionally divisive groups of supporters. When the trustees of the Dallas Museum decided to purchase 8.9 acres in a depleted downtown district in 1977, hiring Barnes to plan and

build on the land, they activated a city power structure concerned over the loss of tax revenues and population in this core area of town. Surprising virtually all learned observers of Texas politics, the city and its major business executives managed to persuade voters to support a series of bills and referendums that imposed strict zoning regulations on a 60-acre site that became known as "the Arts District." The final plan placed the museum on the western edge of this utopian district surveying a sweep of theaters, concert halls, schools, and smaller museums, which will by the

year 2000, it is hoped, completely reverse the outward flow of people and businesses beyond the city's perimeter.

In Dallas the art museum acts as a flagship for urban change, undermining the hallowed separation of art and life as well as the Texas tradition of opposition to zoning and planning. Of course Barnes ignored these broad social implications as a matter of stylistic habit, cloaking his museum in a deliberately modest wrap of soft gray limestone unmarked by a single rhetorical flourish except for the 40-foot-high

45

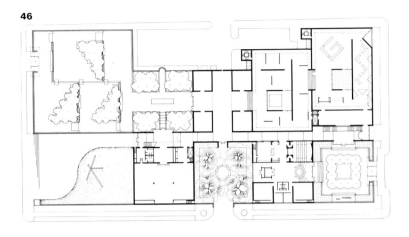

46

45

*Johnson/Burgee
Architects.
Dade County Cultural
Center,
Miami, Florida.
View of facade and
courtyard.*

46

*Edward Larrabee
Barnes/
John M.Y. Lee,
Partners.
Dallas Museum of Art,
Dallas, Texas.
Plan.*

47

*Edward Larrabee
Barnes/
John M.Y. Lee,
Partners.
Dallas Museum of Art,
Dallas, Texas.
Interior of gallery.*

47

barrel vault that rises above the roof at the entrance. The failed rhetoric of the Dallas Museum, which attempts to deny its decisive role in the city and its public support, is yet another sign that the semantic and symbolic representation of the museum's expanded role has yet to be found. In semiotic terms, the signified still eludes its signifier.

Isozaki stumbled into an equally intricate political trap when he accepted the commission to design a brand-new Museum of Contemporary Art for Los Angeles in 1980. The initial energy that generated L.A. MOCA came from a vocal community of younger artists, architects, and collectors, but the crucial step that began to translate the dream into reality was taken by the city. It convinced the developer of a valuable 11.2-acre site in the Bunker Hill section downtown to donate the percentage all new buildings are required to spend on public art to the fledgling museum—a total of $23 million, later supplemented by private contributions. Nevertheless significant control remained in the hands of both the developer and the architecture committee formed by the original organizers. The developer insisted on the uncompromising use of the structural grid envelope imposed by their long-term commercial goals, while the feuding committee objected to scheme after scheme proposed by Isozaki, thirty-six in all. Essentially the committee demanded the very "self-effacing warehouse" that Helen Searing had declared null and void in the eighties and which Isozaki simply refused to deliver. Yet in the end his grander, more decorative scheme prevailed and the committee resigned, rebuked by the trustees and the public. Ironically, the committee's wish was fulfilled by Frank Gehry, the "local" architect whom they originally ignored in favor of Isozaki. Known as the "Temporary Contemporary" and devoted to experimental exhibitions and performances, Gehry's brilliant conversion of an old firehouse near Isozaki's "final" site in 1985 proved in time to exert an abiding hold on the affection of its audience (see Chapter IV) and stands to this day.

48

48
*Arata Isozaki
and Associates.
Museum of Contemporary
Art, Los Angeles.
Aerial view.*

49
*Arata Isozaki
and Associates.
Museum of Contemporary
Art, Los Angeles.
Exterior.*

50
*Arata Isozaki
and Associates.
Museum of Contemporary
Art, Los Angeles.
Interior.*

49

50

Isozaki's richly contoured structure, cloaked in red sandstone from India and prefaced near its barrel-vaulted entrance with a curvaceous white wall (later named after Marilyn Monroe), gratified even its severest critics when it opened. But the "permanent" MOCA bears everywhere the stamp of both the political necessities that brought it to life and the ambivalence of its wry designer. The galleries within are often as wide open and "flexible" in their spacious contours as any loft or as the Miesian-contained volumes in Berlin, although they alternate with closed, well-defined, roomlike spaces. The integrated suspended ceiling flatters the ears of its clientele by toning down the shrill sounds that bounce off its crisp metal-framed interior. In the boardroom beneath the barrel vault that beckons the public into the park, Isozaki and lighting designer Paul Marantz pieced together an intricate series of light sources, which are diffused by a perforated metal ceiling. Encased by lacquer-coated aluminum walls, this beautifully detailed room is clearly intended to lure and flatter the public-spirited collectors upon whom any young fragile museum depends to survive.

Beyond his sleek walls, however, the architect jousts with the meaning of his interior and with his fractious client by covering his roof with pyramids that inevitably recall Egypt and its stark, dry landscape. *Despite my sleek glamour,* says his building, *I am surrounded by a cultural desert.* With this mischievous allusion, Isozaki, unlike Barnes, comments ironically on the conflicting cultural energies at the core

51

of his museum, and of Los Angeles itself, at once the citadel of celluloid, mass-audience culture and an anxious challenger to the fine art hegemony of New York and the old world. Though he fails completely to embody the incurably divided society we inhabit, Isozaki hints, probes, and mocks the condition that gave birth to MOCA, thereby softening its royalist connotations. Isozaki is finally MOCA's sphinx, not its pharaoh.

51
Arata Isozaki and Associates. Museum of Contemporary Art, Los Angeles. Gallery installation with skylight.

52
Arata Isozaki and Associates. Museum of Contemporary Art, Los Angeles. Exterior with courtyard.

52

Behind the Polymorphous Facade: Unity

53
*Louis Kahn,
with Preston M. Gerne
and Associates.
Kimbell Art Museum,
Fort Worth, Texas.
Gallery installation.*

54
*Louis Kahn,
with Preston M. Gerne
and Associates.
Kimbell Art Museum,
Fort Worth, Texas.
Gallery installation.*

While the design of the late twentieth-century museum reflects the tension inherent in its institutional identity, several critical elements tend to link the interior arrangements of the Kimbell Art Museum in Fort Worth, Texas (1972), the Yale Center for British Art, the High, and many of their cousins. Rather than the rigidly symmetrical plan proposed by Durand or the enclosed "room" structure preferred for the emancipated Louvre by the right-wing revolutionaries, the enclosed spaces of these museums embrace diversity. Enclosed rooms alternate with open, loft-style spaces spliced or surrounded by long, broad corridors that nourish circulation. The 40-foot-high ascending corridor that dominates the Dallas Museum is the most dramatic example of this shift. Here, strolling becomes the central pleasure of museum attendance rather than simply means to an end. Here, as in the Kimbell, the High, and most of all, Renzo Piano's Menil Collection opened in Houston in 1987, the museum takes on organic life, its spaces transformed into centers of activity rather than static meditation.

The pronounced presence of natural light in almost all major museums erected during these years reflects deeper, unseen needs as well. Certainly it distinguishes this century's most recent museums from those built earlier, which were primarily committed to artificial illumination: a vivid case in point is the Museum of Modern Art in New York, which insisted both on windowless galleries and low ceilings to approximate the bourgeois living room for which the art displayed there was allegedly made. Here, too, Kahn proves a significant departure. In the Kimbell Art Museum he developed a system of perforated anodized aluminum reflectors, which allowed sunlight to be reflected down from his barrel-vaulted roofs into the galleries at a level far below conventional windows or skylights. This system, widely imitated and modified in the years that followed, permitted certain museums the luxury of using natural light, with its changing, refreshing moods, in all galleries except those reserved for fragile, aging paintings, drawings, or manuscripts. But this conversion was motivated by cultural and social factors as well as technological evolution, for the sun enhanced the pleasure of walking through as well as meditating, dining, and talking in spaces increasingly considered "public," if not festive.

The enormous works of art that now must be contained in the museum, along with its multiplying functional diversity and the increasing size of the audience itself, has meant that scale has also become a point of profound consideration. What is needed is a means of erecting structures that can contain large-scale works as a practical reality rather than a projection of grandiose ambition. At a time when half of all the human beings ever born are alive, the sheer number of visitors daunts our repertoire of signs and structures. The National Air and Space Museum in Wash-

53

54

ington, D.C., opened in 1976 and designed by Hellmuth, Obata, and Kassabaum, attracted one million visitors in its first month, exceeding even the Pompidou Center two years later. Averaging 7.3 million per year, it will certainly pass the figure of 730 million in total attendance by the end of the century. Yet the four marble-faced blocks that confront the public are, like Barnes's stolid Dallas Museum, noncommittal and somber—unlike Pompidou, where vivacity softens scale, or L.A. MOCA, where high wit restrains pretense. Indeed the somber facade of Air and Space seems to contradict its own vast popularity and iconic grandeur of the engines, rockets, missiles, medals, and even the Lindbergh's *Spirit of St. Louis* from 1927 suspended from its ceiling. Yet Air and Space's hulking 200,000 square feet of interior space is not large enough to begin to contain its subject: the fuselage of one Boeing 747 alone is longer than the museum is wide.

55

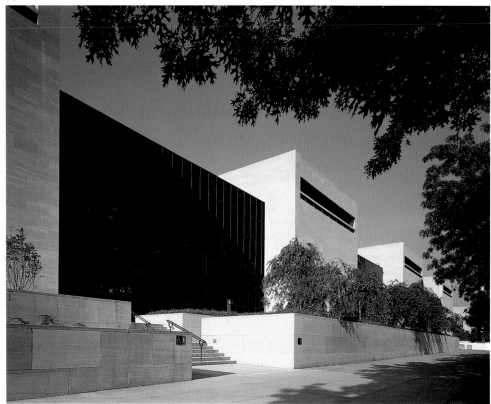

55

*Helmuth, Obata
& Kassabaum.
National Air and Space
Museum,
Smithsonian
Institution,
Washington, D.C.
Exterior.*

56

*Helmuth, Obata
& Kassabaum.
National Air and Space
Museum,
Smithsonian
Institution,
Washington, D.C.
Main entrance hall.*

57

57

*Peter Busmann
and Godfried Haberer.
Museum Ludwig, Cologne,
West Germany,
with the Cologne
Cathedral.*

58

*Peter Busmann
and Godfried Haberer.
Museum Ludwig, Cologne,
West Germany.
Exterior.*

59

*Peter Busmann
and Godfried Haberer.
Museum Ludwig, Cologne,
West Germany.
Interior stairs.*

58

59

Surely the formal reticence of Air and Space as well as its reliance on heavy traditional marble does injustice to its mission. The enormous Museum Ludwig, which opened in Cologne, Germany, in 1986 is similarly handicapped. The largest museum in Europe, it houses the old Wallraf-Richartz Museum and an important collection of twentieth-century art. But the Ludwig crouches beside the grand old medieval cathedral that symbolizes this city like a homely sibling afraid to stand up beside its beautiful sister. While the cathedral is proud and vertical, the Museum Ludwig, wrought by Peter Busmann and Godfried Haberer, is decidedly flat and horizontal, its roof covered with twelve 66-foot-long barrel-vaulted zinc beams running beside each other like trains lined up in a station. The exterior, again, hides the intricate glory of the cavernous interior of more than 150,000 square feet. Divided into galleries and public spaces of varying widths, shapes, and heights, and warmed by sunlight streaming in through an elaborate and expensive triple-glazed roof, this giant cost more than $250 million, an understated estimate and all appropriated from public funds.

What is missing here and in Adrian Fainsibler's enormous Center for Science and Industry, which opened in Paris the same year, is a response by the architect either to the profound complexity of the mega-museum's subject—in this latter case the state of the sciences at the end of this century—or the psyche of its audience, which presumably warms to wit, grace, or at least the innovative character of the museum's subject. Instead, Fainsibler presents only a spherical mirror, blandly reflecting the conventional landscape that surrounds the Center on the outskirts of Paris. Here, as in Washington and in Cologne, the architectural challenge posed by the necessity for an epic scale that is appropriate both for its subject matter and for its demanding public is ignored. Instead, we are provided acres of unmarked, undifferentiated surface, risking—and finally achieving—banality.

With a few significant exceptions architects share Castelli's bewilderment. Although nearly all the major museums reared in the seventies and eighties attempt to provide an alternating pattern of room- and loftlike galleries, few match in mood or spatial complexity the wide-open dynamism of the period's fine art itself. The continued growth of a market for new art forms, which flourished in virtually all Western and postindustrial societies, inspired hordes of competing artists to tackle one new terrain of method or manner after another. Inevitably demanding museum representation, particularly in an era when the availability of "traditional" masterpieces has been limited by an eager buyer's market (see Afterword), their products ranged from minimalism and pop, in Castelli's words, to performance and video, genres in which there is essentially no physical object for collection and display.[15] Beyond that, much of the art produced since the end of the Second World War has taken a critical view of the classical museum's self-proclaimed duty to preserve and glorify single objects or "artist heroes." Though often denied or derided by traditional critics,[16] this strain of contemporary art, like Dada itself, nonetheless persists. The work of a neo-Dada master like Joseph Beuys of West Germany, who delighted in using unorthodox materials like felt and wax and, often hiding his works in gallery niches and corners, avoided conventional wall spaces or podia, challenges the orchestration of interior spaces.

Hans Hollein and, once more, Arata Isozaki, are the only museum architects who have yet managed anything close to a sensitive response to avant-garde contemporary art production. It is no accident that both men are deeply involved in the art world as producers (of their own work) and as confidants of artists, critics, and curators. In the magnificent Stadtisches Museum Abteiburg, opened in 1985 in Mönchengladbach, a small city near Cologne, Hollein sculpted out an obsessive arrangement of galleries that act virtually as negatives for the positive that is the vanguard works displayed within them. A cluster of small, unimpressive buildings connected by dull stone paving surmount the terrace at the top of the hill it inhabits, clad in a variety of suitably discordant materials like marble, stainless steel, and glass. Although this museum is deferential and unresolved in its exterior, which from certain angles is barely visible on the surface of the hill, its interior summarizes in decisive terms the state of the art produced in our time. Down in its heart Hollein's museum takes the viewer on a descending tour through enclosures that are finely tuned to the nuances of its contents. At no point are we reminded of the classical division of spaces recommended by Durand and repeated over and again in a century that has violated these same ideals in art and in life. Hollein gleefully chops and rounds off corners. He breaks

60

Hans Hollein.
Museum of Modern Art,
Mönchengladbach,
West Germany.
Aerial view.

61

Hans Hollein.
Museum of Modern Art,
Mönchengladbach,
West Germany.
View of exterior with
grounds.

61

into walls, opening up unexpected views of other galleries. He plays off voluptuous marble surfaces against metallic corridors, neon lights, and vivid red and blue panels. There is one large rectangular gallery for temporary exhibitions and performance art, and there are two flowing, amoebalike galleries on each level with light gray floors and white ceilings, where restrained art of modest size can be comfortable. In the curvaceous "Amorphous Room," curves and swinging wall elements allow for a proliferation of niches into which sculpture, or even a Beuys spill of fat, can be placed. Down below and up above, we find small square rooms entered always on a diagonal, off the classical center, rooms tuned to the dimensions of intimate works. There is even an "Yves Klein Area" near an intersection of galleries that surrounds a series of steps. The viewer can descend or ascend them, absorbing one gold and four blue paintings by the defiant master of "monochrome adventure," as he described his work.

62

62

Hans Hollein.
Museum of Modern Art,
Mönchengladbach,
West Germany.
Gallery installation.

63

Hans Hollein.
Museum of Modern Art,
Mönchengladbach,
West Germany.
Gallery installation.

64

*Arata Isozaki
and Associates.
Okanoyama Graphic
Art Museum,
Okanoyama, Japan.
Lateral facade.*

65

*Arata Isozaki
and Associates.
Okanoyama Graphic
Art Museum,
Okanoyama, Japan.
Interior with skylight.*

64

66

66
Arata Isozaki
and Associates.
Okanoyama Graphic
Art Museum,
Okanoyama, Japan.
Entrance.

67
Arata Isozaki
and Associates.
Okanoyama Graphic
Art Museum,
Okanoyama, Japan.
Gallery installation.

67

Finally, Hollein provides nothing less than a narrow, wry approximation of a medieval nave in a room called, simply, "the Gallery," which runs from the ground up for two stories and is capped by a mischievous circular skylight. Accessible from a bridge above that appears to connect the two sides of the museum, or by foot, down a deep divide of steps, this room by its nature isolates and enhances any work seen here—from a set of iconic white cubes by American sculptor Bruce Nauman to the stark black *Cloth Picture* by Peter Palermo. The tension created by the open vertical sweep of the ceiling and the confining impact of the tall, narrow, imposing white walls makes this one of the most powerful spaces in our time in which a work of art can hang, or sprawl.

The Mönchengladbach museum imposes both movement and ambiguity upon its public. Nothing is presumed; everything is left open by the vivid contrasts between enclosures. The same can be said of Isozaki's Okanoyama Graphic Arts Museum, situated in a verdant field near a small town in the center of Japan, although its tone is vastly different. Where Hollein is a witty but committed participant in the art displayed in Mönchengladbach, Isozaki is distinctly detached and irreverent in Okanoyama, if affectionate. The museum is totally devoted to the work of one man, the graphic artist Tadanori Yokoo, its founder. Despite the fact that Isozaki is Yokoo's close friend, nowhere in this building does he display anything approaching the bemused reverence that suffuses Mönchengladbach. Informed early on that Japan National Railways meant to build a station beside the future museum, Isozaki plotted a brilliant structural metaphor to accommodate the revised landscape, stretching his museum out beside the station like a train stopped to load passengers. The columned portico entrance hall-cum-locomotive faces north, like the Japan Railway car, and stretched out behind are three "cars," or galleries,

wrapped in yellow stucco with orange-painted circulation spaces between. As it happens, the differing spaces of the three galleries house different aspects of Yokoo's work, which ranges across a variety of media and manners, echoing the modality of Mönchengladbach. Furthermore the concept of the "train" leaves open the possibility of extension beyond the caboose into another decade and another form of expression. In Okanoyama, art has become metaphorically a matter of progress or movement, not finality, mocking (surely intentionally) the classical industrial reference at the head, in the locomotive.

But Isozaki's irreverence does not stop here. In the center of this museum in the center of Japan, the visitor chances upon nothing less than a palm tree rising up from a well cut in the glass-block floor on the gallery level, which we glimpse from above. In one sense the tree is a literal reference to Yokoo's work in the seventies, which often employed images of tropical paradise. But in another sense its living, gently swaying presence mocks the notion of the museum in deadly repose, sitting on timeless treasures. Nor is this the end of mockery: just beyond the palm tree, on the way to the caboose that contains Yokoo's work from the eighties, a skewed pattern of grids has been sketched upon the walls, subtly subverting both the spiral staircase that leads down to the floor below and the doors themselves, which appear off-center to the surprised eye. Nearby, in a working studio that is part of the museum, the walls are cut into sensuous curves that recall yet another of Yokoo's recurrent sixties images, the body of actress Marilyn Monroe. Here, at least, architecture and the avant-garde are in reasonable syncopation, acting as comic partners rather than tragic adversaries.

A sense of humor evokes
what would vanish.
Paradox is used to
make what is invisible,
visible.
—Arata Isozaki,
interview (1988)

While the imperial museum flourished in Europe and the United States during the 1970s and 1980s, in Japan it fragmented and broke into many parts beyond the yoke of unyielding tradition. Although Isozaki's sense of humor and paradox infuses all of his work, back to the Fujimi Country Club House shaped in the form of a question mark (why, indeed, play golf? he asked his clients), it has clearly been provoked by an approach to architecture that encourages design liberation, if not license. Certainly one cannot imagine any "functional" office building, university, or factory indulging the playful geometry evident in two of Isozaki's earlier museums, the Gumma Prefectural Museum (1974) and the Kitakyushu Municipal Art Museum (1975), in which cubes and boxes never quite appear to be solid or centered. Nor is Isozaki alone. Architects as varied in mood and ideology as Kenzo Tange, Fumihiko Maki, Kisho Kurokawa, Hiroshi Hara, Kyono Kikukate, Shozo Uchii, and Kiko Mozuna have unleashed museums that represent formal and philosophical extremes stretching far beyond modernism and postmodernism. In Japan, the museum is as likely to resemble a country villa as it is a rocket ship poised to launch, as likely to rise up in the middle of a bustling department store as on the edge of one of the world's largest marshlands (as in Hokkaido). The Japanese museum may just as probably contain "touch-me" blocks as Zen pottery or Jasper Johns prints, or it may imitate the form of an oblong universe, a three-dimensional mandala, or a red-crested crane as well as a neoclassical temple. Imperialism is absent because coherence is absent.

This condition results from the institutional museum's late arrival in Japan and its rapid multiplication in the 1970s and 1980s. While sacred objects have been preserved and protected for centuries in Japan, the idea of an open public museum did not arise until late in the last century, a consequence of Westernization in many fields.[17] The Tokyo Metropolitan Gallery was erected with great fanfare in 1926 but stood virtually alone until the end of World War II and the onset of rapid social and industrial change. The extraordinary surge of interest in the arts that accompanied rising prosperity led one city and state or prefectural government after another to appease public demand by building "museums." The private sector was equally primed, leading wealthy corporations and individuals alike (some of them artists, like Tadanori Yokoo) to construct new museums. In postindustrial Japan, the creation of a new museum has become as natural and as gratifying as the purchase of a large estate or a rare collection of vintage wine. In the 1950s cultural and science museums opened at the rate of ten a year. By the 1980s, the rate had multiplied many times, with the central government actively encouraging the phenomena with direct grants and by readily approving local bond issues.

68
*Arata Isozaki
and Associates.
Gunma Prefectural
Museum of Fine Arts,
Takasaki, Japan.
Main facade.*

69
*Arata Isozaki
and Associates.
Gunma Prefectural
Museum of Fine Arts,
Takasaki, Japan.
Interior stairway.*

70
*Arata Isozaki
and Associates.
Hara Museum,
Sinagawa Ward,
Japan.
Exterior.*

68

69

71
*Arata Isozaki
and Associates.
Hara Museum,
Sinagawa Ward,
Japan.
Interior.*

72
*Arata Isozaki,
and Associates.
Hara Museum,
Sinagawa Ward,
Japan.
Section drawing.*

72

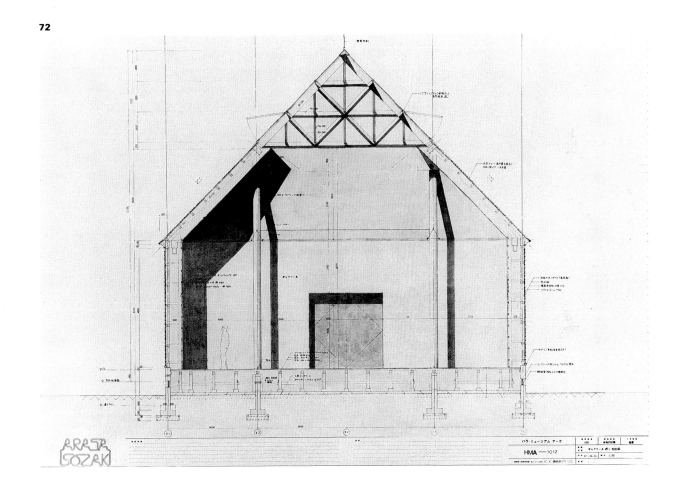

That the museum in Japan often is designed, constructed, and poised to open without any works of art at all to display seems to be a matter of minor importance. Openings are simply delayed while city governments appropriate funds quickly to assemble a collection, or a wealthy benefactor buys a distinguished Millet, Picasso, or Kandinsky just in time, as Japanese critic Hiroshi Sasaki once charged.[18] For the Japanese, clearly, the "museum" is an entirely worldly phenomenon lacking the sacred connotations that prevent American artists or French lingerie stores from naming museums after themselves. Isozaki's whimsy is a direct and refreshing result of this relaxed spirit, as is the metaphysical abandon of an architect like Kiko Mozuna, whose Municipal Museum in Koshiro on the edge of an immense marsh is a three-level spiral-shaped emblem of the three-level universe of heaven, earth, and man.

In Japan the "museum," particularly the "art museum" (or *bijutsukan*), is a distinctly impure phenomenon that can indulge the senses, tickle the comic spirit, proclaim a commercial or mystical program, or simply order or display objects of high elitist concern. The museum in Japan is at once pure and impure, a creature indistinct from what Isozaki himself calls *ma*, or the sense of space always existing in time—that is, of the immateriality of material forms. In Western terms, *ma* refers simply to the incurably existential nature of the museum at the end of this century, redefined every time it is built and opened.

The immense Yokohama City Museum from 1988 by Kenzo Tange, the high modernist father figure for virtually all post-war Japanese architects, is a perfect case in point. The largest art museum in Japan when it opened (93,000 square feet), the towering sliced cylinder that challenges the ocean before it is a giant storage chamber for works of art as yet uncollected in a city that previously had no museum at all. The galleries spread out at the base of this intrepid tribute to unborn treasure in two asymmetrical wings, one circular, one diamond-shaped. Kisho Kurokawa's City Art Museum in Nagoya (1988), another city late to cultivate *bijutsukan*, is multiple in form and reference. No sooner does the viewer enter beneath a clean, rational grid, signaling the modernity of the building and its collection-yet-to-come, than he faces a plethora of images, colors, and forms recalling Japan's past, including a traditional pink lozenge shape circling the ducts of the exhaust pipes, and tall, ramrod steel chairs borrowed from the Edo period that stand in the video gallery. This artificial mixture of contemporary function and historic recall is maintained throughout this museum, forcing past and present into a hard-edged mixture that culminates finally with the roof, where the triple-glazed skylights, anchored by a solid panel that moves by remote control and deftly tunes the level of light, are, of course, formed in patterns that recall the pyramids—this time, alas, without Isozaki's saving self-referential wit.

73

73
Kiko Mozuna.
Kushiro City Museum,
Kushiro, Japan.

74

75

74
Kisho Kurakawa
Architect
and Associates.
Nagoya Municipal
Museum,
Nagoya, Japan.
Overall view.

75
Kisho Kurakawa
Architect
and Associates.
Nagoya Municipal
Museum,
Japan.
South elevation.

76
Kisho Kurakawa
Architect
and Associates.
Nagoya Municipal
Museum,
Japan.
Interior.

76

77

*Kisho Kurakawa
Architect
and Associates.
Nagoya Municipal
Museum,
Japan.
Interior stairway.*

78

*Kisho Kurakawa
Architect
and Associates.
Nagoya Municipal
Museum,
Nagoya, Japan.
Interior.*

77

The Japanese art museum is clearly designed without inhibition, technical or esthetic. The Ken Domon Museum of Photography in Sakata, on the western coast—another gallery devoted entirely to one artist—buries one wing in the foot of a hill to symbolize the timeless quality of Domon's photographs, while the opposite wing is perched just above an artificial lake, which suggests the flow of time captured in his pictures. In Hiroshi Hara's Tazaki Museum in Karuizawa, north of Tokyo, the building salutes itself constantly by stenciling details of its form and interior spaces on windows and glass railings throughout. Given this tendency toward self-glorification, the most successful museums in Japan are usually checked by an inherently self-limiting philosophical or physical concept, as in the Okanoyama Graphic Arts Museum, where narcissism is reined in by wit, or the idyllic Seibu Takanawa Museum by Kiyonori Kikutake, also in Karuizawa (1981). Nestled in the midst of lush, gently rolling grounds, Kikutake's building, commissioned by Seiji Tsutsumi, poet and president of the vigorous Seibu department store chain, is low, peaceful, and serene. Beneath an arched roof with gently overlapping eaves that recalls a traditional tea house expanded to public scale, three long galleries of varying sizes have been created, one of which stretches into a hill and merges the museum almost imperceptibly with the landscape. A Corten steel bridge carries the viewer across a pond into the fields beyond, where the museum's modern sculpture collection is displayed.

Here and in the transparent envelope that is the National Museum of Modern Art in Kyoto, by Fumihiko Maki, we find a delicate potential link between Japan and the West expressed by a new sensibility

78

that is at once richly modern and re-servedly traditional, approaching if not embracing Isozaki's iconoclastic daring. In his essay "The Public Dimension in Contemporary Architecture," Maki unveils the secret to his building in Kyoto:

> *The true essence of Japanese public architecture, I believe, is not to be found in the building . . . but in its space and territory . . . in the sensitivity to borders, both marked and unmarked; in the multiple layering of space by means of* shoji *and their screens; and in the spatial arrangements structured not by the idea of a center but by the idea of depth* (oku).[19]

Yet at first glance his museum is as purely modern as its name. Opened in 1986, it features a collection and exhibition program devoted in part to traditional and regional art as well as contemporary international work, most of all photography. The facade of the museum is a rectilinear glass-and-steel grid, a pure recomposition of Walter Gropius's sturdy Fagus Factory early in this century or the work of De Stijl in Holland in the twenties, relieved only by a gently gabled roof in deference to the ancient heritage of Japan's old capital city. But look again, closely. The simple box-like structure rests on four translucent columns, one in each corner, which reveal vertical stair columns. At night the light radiating from within the corners makes these bewitching shafts more than a match for the giant red *tori* gates to Kyoto itself that rise nearby. But the columns also give the lie to their load-bearing function. Indeed the entire composition of the facade clearly reveals itself to be decorative, down to the gray granite panels that alternate with clear and translucent glass on the south "wall" across the canal. The visitor can at once detect the screenlike or *shoji* quality of this pattern at the corners of the building, where its narrow, thin dimensions are openly confessed.

Inside, the persistent elaboration of space as illusive depth continues. No sooner do we enter the building than we are immediately attracted to the large stairwell that is flooded with light from the skylight at the top of the museum. On bright days the space is as luminous as silver, leading the visitor to ascend the stairs, stopping on the third floor where the exhibition galleries begin, finishing on the fourth floor (where the stairwell does not lead) and the level of illumination drops away from the shining central axis. Inside, the galleries are open and flexible. By pushing most of his circulation—as well as his mechanical "service" systems—to the translucent corners, Maki has freed the interior space for art and meditation. It is a splendid if slightly flawed museum: the truncation of the skylit stairwell before the top floor deprives the public of the full vertical sweep promised in the lobby below and implicit in the open airy insubstantiality that characterizes this building. This insubstantiality sets it apart from virtually all recent structures in Japan and elsewhere, with the exception of the extraordinary Spiral Building in Tokyo, also designed by Maki, the mixed-use quality of which (commercial and "museum" functions are intertwined) makes it critical to our later discussion in Chapter V. In Kyoto the museum comes playfully and seductively to terms with the materialism of its own time. Of course its denial of volume, weight, and solidity is a hoax: the steel, load-bearing frame of the Kyoto museum rests securely in the earth. But Maki's fantasy prefers to pretend to be something else, beyond itself, and beyond even the art it conceals and reveals.

80

81

80
*Fumihiko Maki
and Associates.
National Museum
of Modern Art,
Kyoto, Japan.
Interior stairway.*

81
*Fumihiko Maki
and Associates.
National Museum
of Modern Art,
Kyoto, Japan.
Interior.*

82
*Fumihiko Maki
and Associates.
National Museum
of Modern Art,
Kyoto, Japan.
Gallery installation.*

82

Again the Question: How Can Imperialism <u>Face</u> *the World?*

We have seen that the robust growth of museums of all kinds near the end of this century has not resolved the critical issue of their signification in architecture. The inherent Western need to elevate or ennoble the art museum in particular has led many architects to revive classical or Renaissance motifs, most of all the once-rejected notion of the interior as a sequential series of palatial rooms arranged around a central axis. But the imperialist libido intrinsic to what came to be known as postmodernism is implicit as well in the grandiose technology of core moderns like Mies, whose New National Gallery in Berlin, his last major building, simply resolved his lifelong quest for the perfect, seemingly illimitable space-frame pavilion; what's more, it is mounted, as already noted, on precisely the same sort of podium as Schinkel's explicitly decorative Altes Museum. The self-effacing warehouse rejected by so many architects and critics in this period was hardly shy about asserting its own pompous bulk, as we have seen in Hellmuth, Obata, and Kassabaum's Air and Space Museum, or, when possible, its gleaming metallic finish, as in Norman Foster's Sainsbury Centre, constructed in England in 1977. Neither the warehouse ideal nor its myriad opposites has been able to resolve the gap between outside and inside, between the face it presents to the world and the mind-numbing complexity of the spaces and functions within—to say nothing of the museum's strangely balanced sources of support, at once public and private, vulgar and elitist, traditional and avant-garde. Veteran museum director Charles Cunningham's angry outburst at a high-level conference on the future of his profession, inspired by his distaste for the multiplicity of services museums now offer, aptly summarizes the frustration implicit in the failure of contemporary architects to resolve the age-old challenge of their art: to pair inside and out, back and front, face and function.

Beyond Schinkel and Mies, architects such as Henry Cobb of I. M. Pei and Partners and Frank Gehry have reached for museum forms that explicitly proclaim their face-saving functions. In Cobb's Portland (Maine) Museum of Art (1982), which gracefully bestrides an irregular squarish site, the face steps out from the main body of the museum and declares itself to be precisely that—a symbolic front. At the top of an indigenous waterstruck redbrick wall, a "screen" is cut into alternating incised circles and squares. These cutouts refer directly to the variegated spatial ordering of the galleries

83

84

84
Frank O. Gehry
& Associates.
Aerospace Museum,
Los Angeles.
Exterior.

85
Frank O. Gehry
& Associates.
Aerospace Museum,
Los Angeles.
Detail of exterior.

85

within, but they also serve (as does the wall itself) as an openly declared act of ornamentation.[21] Gehry's Aerospace Museum in Los Angeles, on the other hand, is a blunt signifier for its subject. Across the galvanized metal building's side facade the architect has suspended a Lockheed F-104 Starfighter. In terms popularized in the last decade by Robert Venturi, the Aerospace Museum seems at first glance to be the perfect example of what has come to be called "the decorated shed," a building whose face cosmeticizes and contradicts the reality within, as is often the case with brilliantly lit and embellished diners or gas stations. But Gehry's Starfighter errs only on the side of integrity. His suspended airplane perfectly summarizes the museological contents within, if not the disposition of its tiny, cramped, vertical galleries, its gantrylike viewing tower, or the contradictory needs of its public, at once lured to the glamour of flight and repelled by the destructive uses to which it has occasionally been put in this century. The Aerospace Museum is, rather, a decorated mirror of itself, not a shed.

86
Frank O. Gehry
& Associates.
Aerospace Museum,
Los Angeles.
Interior.

87

89

James Stirling,
Michael Wilford
& Associates.
Staatsgalerie,
Stuttgart,
West Germany.
View into courtyard.

90

James Stirling,
Michael Wilford
& Associates.
Staatsgalerie,
Stuttgart,
West Germany.
Detail of courtyard.

90

Certainly the most consistently praised new museum to appear in the 1980s was James Stirling and Michael Wilford's Staatsgalerie in Stuttgart, which raised the possibility that here at last is an edifice that gives a total account of itself. Unlike either Cobb's screen wall or Gehry's airborne facade, however, the face of the Staatsgalerie is almost impossible to "read." In fact the Staatsgalerie is perhaps properly perceived as a single face that dons several masks, depending upon the approach or disposition of the viewer. There is no central, well-defined entrance to the Stuttgart museum but instead a magnanimous ramp that circles around the U-shaped core, allowing the visitor to enter, circle, or ascend the museum to the very top. These multiple modalities are reinforced by the spectacular array of clashing materials and colors that enliven the exterior and much of the interior. Stirling's museum wraps itself alternatively in coats of low-born stucco, large undulating sheets of glass punctuated by blatantly industrial steel beams, and reinforced concrete spliced with high-born travertine and granite bands, which often appear—falsely—to be protruding into space. Indeed close up this apparently stolid classical masonry wall cheerfully acknowledges that it is a mere skin—like Maki's gridded panels in Kyoto—by uncaulking its joints and revealing the thinness of the skin. There is barely a corner on the Staatsgalerie where the eye can rest without instantly glimpsing a distracting curve, rise, or gap around the next cheek, not to mention color shifts of mounting intensity—most of all in the succulent steel handrails that ring the spiraling ramp, now painted crayon blue, now pink, now yellow, and most of all, bold green, the very shade that drenches the tall steel columns enfolded with undulating glass.

91
James Stirling,
Michael Wilford
& Associates.
Staatsgalerie,
Stuttgart,
West Germany.
Exterior.

The Staatsgalerie proves as well to be honeycombed with historical references (to Schinkel's Altes Museum, of course, to Rome, to Corbusier), leading to the assertion that it sums up the postmodern esthetic at its zenith. Certainly the interior galleries, laid out on three rising floors beyond the sinuous, curving glass lobby, appear to follow classical and palatial models, with oversize doorways, mock pediments, and broadly beveled frames. But Stirling's heavy, muscular building exudes a modern industrial panache in its frankly exposed steel beams, high pop colors, and joyous indulgence in clear glass. Often the architect twits history in the parodic Isozakian manner, avoiding the solemn reverence that characterizes much postmodern design. Stirling mounts solemn cornice fragments on steel beams in the corners of closed "classical" rooms. Most of all, he installs a voluptuously curved outdoor gallery in the "center" of his complex, a gallery directly resembling a Roman pantheon but one conspicuously lacking an icon or symbol in the middle: in brief, a decentralized center.

Surely Stirling's multivalent mode of attack, not to mention his double-coded reading of the past/present, is directly responsible for the popularity of the Staatsgalerie and for the misinterpretation of its supposed fealty to tradition. Lacking an identifiable face and rejecting an axial center, it allows for multiple, even clashing, interpretations and uses. Thoroughly ambiguous and therefore contemporary in mood, it brilliantly poses architectonic questions that are never, finally, answered.

92

James Stirling,
Michael Wilford
& Associates.
Staatsgalerie,
Stuttgart,
West Germany.
Interior.

Universality, at Last, Reaches Its End

The museum is bad because it does not tell the whole story.
—Le Corbusier, "Other Icons: The Museums," in The Decorative Art of Today *(1924)*

We have forgotten that the impetus for what Carol Duncan and Alan Wallach call the incurably ideological "universal survey museum" is quintessentially modern. Stemming from the desire to enfold all knowledge within a single book or building and dating back to Diderot's *Encyclopédie* in its earliest manifestations, this dream has finally become credible in this century when the means of copying and distributing facts, thoughts, and images has reached the speed of light. Nietzsche portrayed modern man in an esthetic garden, "surrounded with all the styles and arts of all time, so that like Adam with the beasts he might give them a name." The encyclopedic Smithsonian Institution in Washington, D.C., and the massive Metropolitan Museum in New York City are logical outgrowths of this libidinous intellectuality, as is Mies's dream of a lighter-than-air suspended ceiling stretching into infinity or an infinitely open, flexible spatial envelope posing as a limitless gallery. Corbusier demanded without the slightest hesitation that the museum collect and exhibit everything; as it is, he argued, the museum shows us only the objects preserved by the elite, ignoring the poor, the downtrodden, the "garbage." Let us have instead everything, he asked in his proposal for a museum of unlimited growth in 1939.

But the thirst for encyclopedic presentation has an analogue in another need, one inherent in the personalization and dissemination of knowledge represented by public museums, book, radio, television, audiotape, videotape. We need as well in the post-Enlightenment era a sense of access, or ease in the approach to knowledge and to architecture. The often-expressed sense of relief effected by the seminal museums designed by Louis Kahn in Fort Worth, Texas, and New Haven, Connecticut, is a direct reflection of this need. Though the Kimbell and Kahn's two Yale galleries are endowed with thousands of precious art objects, and though they make use of the most advanced methods of construction and lighting, ultimately their success lies in the fact that their users find them uniquely comfortable. The Kahn museums are always saturated with natural light. The Center for British Art is entered through a four-story white-oak-paneled lobby that rises up through the entire structure, visible from all floors, galleries, and windows and unlocks the formal gestalt of the structure. If Kahn's museums do not tell "the whole story," as Corbusier irrationally demanded, they at least tell the truth about themselves, easing our souls as we use them.

93

94

93
Louis Kahn.
Center for British
Studies,
Yale University.
Interior with gallery
and stairwell.

94
Louis Kahn.
Center for British
Studies,
Yale University.
Gallery installation.

Imperialism, Too, Finds Its Antithesis

There is something about a building which is different from a painting: when a building is being built, there is an impatience to bring it into be-ing. . . . Look at the building after it is built. Each part . . . tries to say "when you're using the build-ing let me tell you about how I was made."
—Louis Kahn, quoted in Conversations with Architects *(1973)*

Such a plan is one whose parts work so precisely together that nothing essential can be moved without throwing the ensemble into disarray.
—Karl Friedrich Schinkel, Sammlung architektonischer Entwurfe *(1866)*

Kahn's museums, methods, and theories are the proper antidote to the imperial mu-seum and certainly to the notion that the "art" of architecture resides in the articu-lation of the structure or in historical recall as its own end, unrelieved by wit, temporal reference, or museological purpose, which is of course the transmission of knowl-edge. If Kahn had no sense of face or frontal signification, he at least knew how to turn the focus of the public inward to-ward the subject matter, secure in a sense of how the building is made. For all its physical splendor and tempering wit, the Staatsgalerie nonetheless insists on an out-ward focus, on itself rather than its pur-pose: the pantheon at the center is vacant because the architect has no desire to fill it. The prototypical museum envisioned and realized by Kahn is, in contemporary terms, like a television screen, whereas the Staatsgalerie, the best of its kind, is the television set or frame.

In the middle of 1987, Renzo Piano of Italy, codesigner of the Pompidou Cen-ter, unveiled the Menil Collection, a mu-seum in Houston, Texas, that broke so sharply with his own past and with the styl-istic exuberance of his colleagues that it baffled the critical fraternity and the pro-fession. "Overwhelmingly nonmonumen-tal," quipped one commentator. The building's purpose was to enclose the be-loved body of modern art assembled by John and Dominique de Menil over de-cades of impassioned collecting, yet merge into the residential neighborhood that sur-rounded. This double, almost contradic-

95

96

tory goal led the architect toward his final, nearly invisible form. Piano responded by clothing the 100,000-square-foot, steel-frame structure in soft cypress wood siding painted gray to blend with the sedate surrounding neighborhood. Approached from the street, indeed, the museum seems at first glance nothing more than a rusticated, block-long, three-and-a-half story family mansion surrounded by a wide white porch. The leaflike forms that fringe the unassuming flat roof and the porch appear to be pleasantly decorative, lending the entire "house" a hint of floral charm.

97

96

Renzo Piano Architects.
Menil Collection,
Houston, Texas.
Detail of exterior.

97

Renzo Piano Architects.
Menil Collection,
Houston, Texas.
Roof trusses.

98

Renzo Piano Architects.
Menil Collection,
Houston, Texas.
Design drawings for
roof trusses.

98

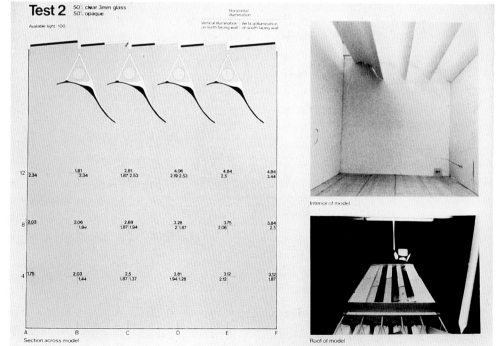

99

Renzo Piano Architects.
Menil Collection,
Houston, Texas.
Gallery installation.

100

Renzo Piano Architects.
Menil Collection,
Houston, Texas.
Interior view of tribal
galleries.

101

Renzo Piano Architects.
Menil Collection,
Houston, Texas.
Plan.

Unlike the imperial museum, however, the Menil Collection grows in stature when entered and examined. The leafy forms reveal themselves to be trusses made of ferro-concrete and ductile iron. There are hundreds of them lurking beneath a roof that is largely made of clear and glazed glass and forms a totally functional "servant" ceiling, much like the mechanized roof of Kahn's first Yale Art Gallery in 1961. The triangulated trusses are tiny, curved marvels of diffraction and reflection. There are so many of them, each one programmed by computer to bend with the exact angle of the sun moving in the Texas sky, that they permit nearly all of the galleries to be totally illuminated by natural light, an achievement unmatched anywhere else, even in Kahn's meticulously designed Kimbell Museum in Fort Worth, where artificial light constantly moderates the effects of the sun. This concept guides the interior as well as the exterior form of

the first "sun-shaded" museum. The black-stained floor in the corridor that runs the entire 500-foot length of the building carries the viewer from one cool, exquisite, high-ceiling gallery to another, each one bathed in serene, sparkling light that changes with the passage of a cloud from one moment to the next. Though the light is frequently dimmer in pure wattage than other museums' artificial illumination, the iris adjusts as it might on a shaded porch, and few observers remember their viewing of the Menil Collection as anything but radiantly clear.

In almost every sense the Menil Collection is a masterpiece. At once radical and conservative, epic and comfortable, hard and soft, it resolves a number of the contradictions at war in the museums of the past decade. While the application of classical reference would have destroyed both its logic and its coherence, the building's parts work together as precisely as Schinkel recommended. Virtually nothing could be thrown away without destroying the entire ensemble, certainly not the leafy trusses that convert the interior into a container not of its own formal exuberance but of light and art. All the Menil collection lacks is a message about its subject: the raging, violent world of the art produced in this century. But Piano's gently rounded structure survives its inherent contradiction.

99

101

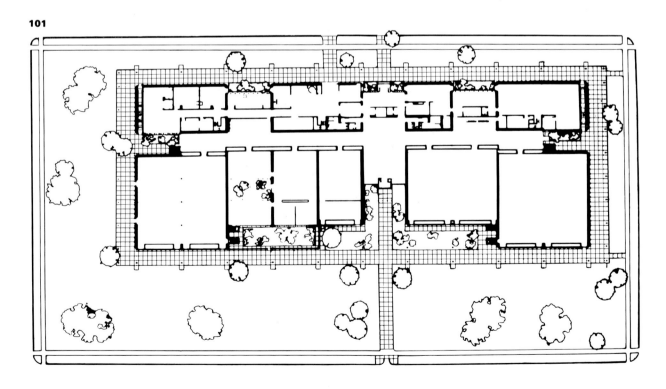

Chapter Four   A D D I N G ,   R E C L A I M I N G ,   R E V I S I N G :
T H E   M U S E U M   G R O W S

102
Aerial view of the
Metropolitan Museum
of Art, New York.

Our building is an attempt to go back to the original model. Ideally, when you go through the museum, it will be difficult to tell at what point in history the different buildings were constructed. It might even be possible to perceive ours as the initial building, and the other as a large addition to it, if it works correctly.
—Thomas Beeby, interview (1988)

How do you make something new that ties into the old? Especially when the old is not necessarily that old? How do you stitch those things together so that the new part has an identity of its own, but an identity that is secondary to the old, even when the new part is many times larger?
—Cesar Pelli, interview (1984)

Seen from the street, the Metropolitan Museum of Art in New York is a vision of classical, ordered serenity. From north to south, its gray Italian Renaissance arcade stretches 1,100 feet down Fifth Avenue, almost masking the differing hands of its several architects. In 1893 Calvert Vaux designed the original building, then set back far off the Avenue like a tiny Greek Revival temple sited in sylvan surroundings, followed in 1905 by Richard Morris Hunt, who covered Vaux's structure with imposing columns and a portico—the central entrance gallery that still commands the eye. The stately firm of McKim, Mead, and White followed shortly after, in 1912–13, adding two wings with a similar presence and similar historical references. But the apparent coherence is essentially artifice and illusion. Inside, the Metropolitan Museum is sheer stylistic anarchy, one disparate gallery ceding to another, as lively and informal as the masses who gather on the steps at high noon ringed by vendors, mimes, dancers, and guitar players.

From an aerial view the Metropolitan is revealed as an architectural form that knows no precedent, either in history or in geometry. Spreading out over four huge city blocks, the Met is a multiringed complex of additions without a center, covered by flat modern shells merging into traditional pitched roofs, squat crisscrossed neoclassical boxes, and glass-and-steel pyramids. Hidden deep down in what remains of the "center" is the arched Greek Revival roof of Vaux's half-forgotten gal-

103
*Hardy Holzman Pfeiffer
Associates.
Addition to the
Virginia Museum of
Fine Art,
Richmond, Virginia.
Interior.*

104
*Hardy Holzman Pfeiffer
Associates.
Addition to the
Virginia Museum of
Fine Art,
Richmond, Virginia.
Model, north wing.*

lery, visible only from the sky. Formally, the Met is best compared to a network of underground vines, each reaching out past the other toward light, air, and the world beyond on Fifth Avenue.

Yet this asymmetrical agglomeration is as accurate a symbol of the museum at the end of the twentieth century as the monolithic Pompidou in Paris or the Staatsgalerie in Stuttgart. In Europe and most of all in the United States, the mu-

seum has become an additive creature. As the time passes when new structures are generated on open urban and suburban plots, the museum turns organic, adding arms, legs, and—in its newfound appetite for cafes and restaurants—even stomachs. In city after city the crisis is similar, as is the resolution: the scarcity of desirable land combined with the overcrowding of familiar, even beloved buildings dictates expansion rather than removal and replacement.

But specific solutions to this complex social and formal problem vary widely. They begin with the uninhibited indulgence of stylistic pluralism we see at the Met as well as at the Virginia Museum of Fine Arts in Richmond, which raced through four wings following hard upon the appearance of the Neo-Georgian "original" in 1936, ending, for the moment, with a

105

106

quiet buff-colored limestone west wing by Hardy, Holzman, Pfeiffer in 1987. The Des Moines Art Center, another striking example, has somehow artfully blended a neoclassical core by Eliel Saarinen, an expressive modern sculpture gallery by I. M. Pei, and a pristine porcelain enameled steel gallery and restaurant by Richard Meier, the last added in 1985.

In each of these complexes three or more architects have fashioned extensions that often bear little resemblance to the "center" over periods ranging from forty to seventy-five years. But the Los Angeles County Museum of Art (LACMA) achieved discordance on a similar scale in barely three decades. Opened in 1965 in a garish triplex of pseudoclassical boxes designed by William Pereira, LACMA hired Hardy, Holzman, Pfeiffer in 1981 literally to cover up the museum's origins by rearing in the front of its Wilshire Boulevard plot yet another ungainly sight: the 300-foot long, 100-foot high Robert Anderson Gallery, a razor-edged modernist glass box laced with horizontal bands of limestone, green terracotta, and porcelain metal panels.

LACMA's brash discordance defines the extreme pole of carefree eclectic patching. At the farther end, painstaking attempts to meld new and old have produced such projects as Robert Venturi's Sainsbury Wing in London's National Gallery, which playfully appropriates elements of William Wilkins's soft gray porticoed and pillared 1838 "original". The most successful of all is Chicago's Art Institute, where each chop or growth has been crafted to meld into a Beaux Arts structure from 1893 that hovers over Michigan Avenue. The "final stage" of the Art Institute includes the immense South Building added in 1988 by Hammond, Beeby, and Babka, whose newness is nearly imperceptible; indeed the South Building is so exact in its identification that it occasionally appears, on an overcast day, to predate its ancestor.

Between the poles represented by LACMA and Chicago lie a variety of divergent approaches to the genre of architectural addition. I. M. Pei in both the Museum of Fine Arts in Boston and the East Building of the National Gallery in Washington, D.C., and James Stirling in the Clore Gallery of the Tate Museum in London and the Arthur Sackler Gallery pinned on the Fogg Art Museum at Harvard University chose to juxtapose such dissimilar styles of new and old architecture that they appear unified by their very opposition, like two close friends dressed for dinner in deliberately contrasting colors. Pei's barrel-vaulted box lying to the west of Boston's Beaux Arts museum complex from 1909, along with his theatrically knife-edged triangle standing to the east of John Russell Pope's classical National Gallery are both so self-contained they scarcely disturb their partners, much like the pyramid he has planted in the midst of the Louvre. Stirling's orange and buffstone Sackler Gallery from 1985 gestures wildly in the postmodern manner toward the past, but on so many levels it often seems to caricature itself—particularly in the fat concrete "pillars" framing the entrance. These pillars mark the Sackler off from virtually all of the surrounding university, including the old Fogg opened in 1893. Stirling's double-edged Clore Gallery in London (1987) blends at one end into the stonework, cornice, and color of the traditional Tate, while at the other it suddenly adopts glass and steel panels, declaring itself contemporary and apart.

I.M. Pei and Partners.
East Building of the
National Gallery
of Art,
Washington, D.C.
Interior of atrium.

107

108
James Stirling,
Michael Wilford
& Associates.
Clore Gallery addition
to the Tate Gallery,
London.
Entrance.

109
James Stirling,
Michael Wilford
& Associates.
Clore Gallery addition
to the Tate Gallery,
London.
Entrance.

110
James Stirling,
Michael Wilford
& Associates.
Clore Gallery addition
to the Tate Gallery,
London.
Interior.

108

109

110

111
*Richard Meier &
Partners.
Museum for the
Decorative Arts,
Frankfurt,
West Germany.
Main entrance.*

112
*Richard Meier &
Partners.
Museum for the
Decorative Arts,
Frankfurt,
West Germany.
Detail of entrance.*

113
*Richard Meier &
Partners.
Museum for the
Decorative Arts,
Frankfurt,
West Germany.
Exterior courtyard.*

111

112

113

114

115

Richard Meier's delicate Museum for the Decorative Arts in Frankfurt employs a design strategy of extreme contrasts, like LACMA but with much more success. Asked essentially to explode a tiny nineteenth-century villa on the south bank of Frankfurt's Main River, Meier created a colossus that dwarfs but still acknowledges its origin. His three-story, 110,500-square-foot extension of the villa is faced with white porcelain panels and aluminum-framed windows that repeat the fenestration of their predecessor.

Frank Gehry's galvanized metal Aerospace Museum in Los Angeles (1985) is a particularly dramatic echo of Meier's Frankfurt museum. It both replaces and echoes a squat, antiquated armory with a distorted box that resembles an airplane hangar. On its exterior, Gehry hangs nothing less than a Lockheed F-104 Starfighter. At the Hood Museum of Art at Dartmouth College, Charles Moore has created a bold contrast to the older buildings nearby with a comfortable shed-roofed red brick building. Moore's structure acts as an intermediary linking two dramatically opposite neighbors, one gently Neo-Georgian, the other a feisty modern gallery devoted to contemporary art. The Hood itself resembles neither in style but suits both, in scale and in presence.

The Museum of Modern Art in New York opted for a radical revision of its dark interior entrance with a transparent garden wall designed by Cesar Pelli, although it retained its "original" patterned grid-and-glass exterior. Both the Museum of Fine Art in Houston and the Walker Art Center in Minneapolis have permitted themselves arcadian enlargements, in effect, by adding immense sculpture gardens dotted with enormous works of art and interlaced oases of trees, grass, and fountains. But the Jewish Museum in New York permitted itself nothing. In the plans devised in 1988 for doubling its gallery space Kevin Roche, the Metropolitan's guiding hand, proposed that the Jewish Museum move northward into a tiny open space created by destroying the bland, boxlike structure that once sat there. In its place Roche offered nothing less than a Siamese twin of the original, directly copying the fussy French Gothic chateau from 1909 in which the Jewish Museum had been illogically quartered since 1947. Here, perhaps, the architecture of revision nears invisibility.

What might be called "recycling" is another strategy clearly related to the phenomenon of endless additions even when it occasionally involves the creation of entirely new museums. The San Antonio, Texas, Museum of Art decided in 1980 to expand *into* an aging local icon—the Lone Star Brewery, a huge brick Romanesque warehouse in the center of the old city. The Brewery has now been recycled into a cultural palace, forsaking (or simply extending) its commercial origins. When the Los Angeles Museum of Contemporary Art

116
*Charles W. Moore
and Chad Floyd
of Centerbrook
Architects.
Hood Museum of Art,
Dartmouth College,
Hanover, New
Hampshire.
Facade.*

117
*Charles W. Moore
and Chad Floyd
of Centerbrook
Architects.
Hood Museum of Art,
Dartmouth College,
Hanover, New
Hampshire.
Interior stair.*

116

found itself delayed in the construction of its $22 million home (designed by Arata Isozaki) in Bunker Hill Park, it commissioned Frank Gehry to renovate two aging warehouses on a dead-end street, creating the beloved Temporary Contemporary that still stands today. Gehry's design indulges the wide-open spaces and generous daylight pouring in from the warehouses' large overhead windows to display new and unconventional art.

In Venice, the Fiat Corporation converted the Palazzo Grassi, an aging palace on the Grand Canal, into yet another ultra-modern showplace for contemporary art. While the exterior structure was carefully preserved down to the last arch and lintel by Antonio Foscari in 1986, its interior was ironically designed with a spartan modern eye by Gae Aulenti, the despoiler of the Gare d'Orsay in Paris. In Madrid, the city's huge general hospital, built in 1788, was saved from destruction in 1987 when it was given over to the display of art. The "new" Reina Sofia Art Center, 300,000 square feet of space and six cavernous stories high, offers a catacomb of broad, sweeping floors filled with white vaulted galleries devoted to works of art of immense size. In its early years Reina Sofia was able to present comprehensive exhibitions devoted to collectors like Giuseppe Panza di Biumo of Italy and Ray Nasher of the United States, whose tastes emphasize works of massive sculpture that can rarely be seen in their totality.

But recycling reached its fullest expression in the German Architectural Museum in Frankfurt where, near Meier's masterful extension of a villa for the Museum for the Decorative Arts, Mathias Ungers gutted yet another villa, this one

118

built in 1901. Around the old facade, which he has left virtually intact, Meier has established a totally new facade, creating a "house within a house" structure instantly perceptible to the visitor. At the entrance one crosses a red sandstone arcade that matches the exterior of the old villa. Inside, the old villa rises almost to the top of the new structure, stopping at at the attic level where its gabled roof holds museum offices and archives. Here the old core in effect acts as an extension of the new shell.

118
Frank O. Gehry
& Associates.
"Temporary" Los Angeles
Museum of Contemporary
Art, Los Angeles.
Exterior.

119
Frank O. Gehry
& Associates.
"Temporary" Los Angeles
Museum of Contemporary
Art, Los Angeles.
Gallery installation.

119

120
O.M. Ungers.
German Architectural
Museum, Frankfurt,
West Germany.
Main facade.

121
O.M. Ungers.
German Architectural
Museum, Frankfurt,
West Germany.
Detail of facade.

122
O.M. Ungers.
German Architecture
Museum, Frankfurt,
West Germany.
Interior.

120

121

122

123

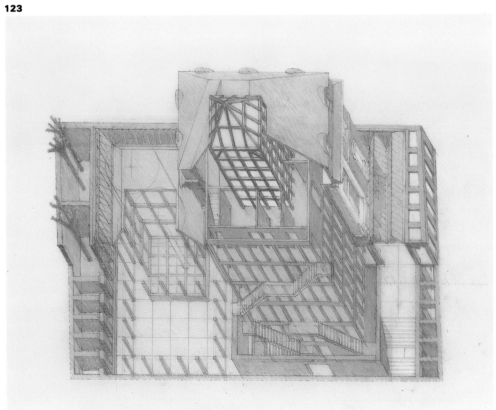

The Psychic Politics of Renewal

When I was asked in 1970 to plan a series of wings on the garden side of the Metropolitan, I decided to turn away from the Fifth Avenue side, which was a mixture of many different styles, and adopt the model of the Botanical Gardens in Washington, D.C. I wanted all the new wings to be faced with glass and slope out toward the landscape, becoming essentially a glass architecture, a gentle greenhouse effect.
—Kevin Roche, interview (1987)

Though essentially pragmatic in its motivation, the idea that the museum should spread its wings rather than build anew was powerfully influenced throughout the seventies and eighties by postmodern revivalism. The notion that the past presented an almost irreproachable value—that old wings should not be touched—lurked behind many disjointed creations. Kevin Roche's valiant plan to link all the wings he was assigned to design at the Metropolitan beginning in 1970 was quite exceptional. His charges ranged from the new American Wing to the Temple of Dendur, which houses an ancient Egyptian sphinx, to the Douglas Dillon Galleries for Chinese Painting. While he was defeated in the end by the inherent contradiction between the Egyptian, American, and Chinese cultures he was asked to blend, Roche at least perceived the threat lurking behind mindless revivalism. Preservation at all costs has left us with a series of grotesque mixed metaphors, featuring endless walls of exposed brick—witness San Antonio's brewery-dressed-for-culture. But it has generated as well a stubborn refusal to link recycling or reconversion to contemporary needs. Reina Sofia's endless procession of similarly scaled white-toned rooms is typical: perfectly suited for hospital use, these spaces are deadly when viewed over and over as a setting for art.

By now it is clear that the need to match form, or period, with content, or use, so evident in the perfect match be-

tween Gehry's Temporary Contemporary and its subject, was barely considered as the contemporary museum began to add wing after wing, moving from its first- and second-generation roots into the late twentieth-century world. Neither did many directors, trustees, or architects anticipate the full-throated roars that often accompanied revision and expansion. Opposition to extensions at the National Gallery in London's Trafalgar Square, LACMA, the Guggenheim, the Whitney, and elsewhere was intense, persistent, and often successful. Throughout the seventies and eighties each of these institutions confronted public criticism virtually on a daily basis. In London a series of competitions and design decisions for the National Gallery were greeted with sarcasm and vitriol, most of all in 1981 when Prince Charles himself termed a starkly modern gallery and office complex by a British firm "a monstrous carbuncle on the face of a much-loved friend," leading the gallery to abandon the project.

Venturi's gentle resolution of the esthetic issues implied by the "old friend" proved that the British public had been primarily offended by the character of the extension, not by the process of modification itself. But in New York the mere idea of touching, not to mention revising, Frank Lloyd Wright's spiral-ramped Guggenheim and Marcel Breuer's jagged, heroic Whitney offended hundreds of thousands of citizens. The early public hearings on both proposals were jammed with opponents as well as supporters. Though the

124
*Kevin Roche
and John Dinkeloo.
Sackler Wing of the
Metropolitan Museum
of Art, New York—
Temple of Dendur.*

125
*Kevin Roche
and John Dinkeloo.
Charles Englehard Court
of the American Wing,
Metropolitan Museum
of Art, New York.*

partisans of Wright and Breuer were enraged on esthetic grounds—neither plan seemed to pay the original proper homage—the critical factor for the public clearly was scale. The first proposal by Gwathmey Siegel & Associates for an eleven-story office and storage tower on the north end of the Guggenheim's site was intended for precisely the same location where Wright himself once planned a high-rise tower to house artists. But Gwathmey-Siegel Plan I allowed the green-tiled tower to cantilever forward to a position at mid-point of the great, haloed Wright rotunda itself. Rather than beholding the dramatic Wright composition isolated in the void, charged critics, we would be confronted with Gwathmey Siegel's cantilevered rectangle hovering over sacred space.

126

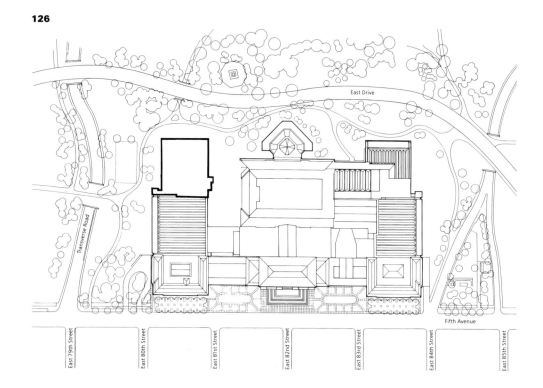

126
Kevin Roche and John Dinkeloo. Plan of the Lila Acheson Wallace Wing, Metropolitan Museum of Art, New York.

127
Venturi, Rauch & Scott Brown. Sainsbury Wing addition to the National Gallery, London. Model.

Michael Graves's gray-and-pink granite Whitney I infuriated press and public for precisely the same reason. Decorative and fanciful, Graves's addition committed the unpardonable sin of more than doubling the old Whitney's size, rising 204 feet above the Breuer building and linking the two facades with a muscular cylindrical hinge that protruded out onto the sidewalk 30 feet beyond the original building—the most offensive bulge of all.

Only when Guggenheim I and Whitney I reduced their proportions—not their style or polemic content—did they ultimately prevail, gaining a series of approvals from courts and zoning commissions alike, as well as measured public support. Gwathmey-Siegel gave up their cantilever and offered instead a slimmer tower that did not dare to break the void above Wright's rotunda. Graves shrank the height of his upper section by 40 percent and the bulk of his impudent hinge to the point that it almost lined up with the Breuer facade. Neither Guggenheim II or

the several subsequent Whitney proposals provided as much space as either institution desperately required, but the functional needs of either museum were rarely attended in the public debate. Overused and overextended, neither the Guggenheim nor the Whitney was able to display more than a fraction of its collection or provide adequate storage, theater, and library facilities. By ignoring the museum as function as well as the museum as style, the opposition thrived. Gwathmey-Siegel and Graves in fact directly contradicted each other stylistically, the former distinctly modernist in its formal vocabulary, the latter a freewheeling postmodern historicist. They erred only because, along with their patrons, they ignored—at first—the museum's inextricable place in the psychic, political, and ceremonial life of the contemporary city.

128

The only art collection in America indisputably more important is that of the Metropolitan Museum in New York. . . . It may be mentioned that there are several pictures in the collection for which $30,000 or $40,000 was actually paid, and many that cost $10,000, $15,000 and $20,000. . . . The collection of modern and contemporary paintings in the Art Institute surpasses in range and value any similar collection in Europe.
—William French (1900)

Enthusiasm, aesthetic curiosity, and tolerance abetted, it must be confessed, by some snobbery and speculation, have gone far in transforming the position of the modern artist, closing that breach of misunderstanding and mutual indifference that had come between him and his public, though in a manner very different from that which existed before the nineteenth century.
—Alfred Barr, "A New Museum" (1929)

There are two causes of Beauty—natural and customary. Natural is from Geometry, consisting of Uniformity . . . and Proportion. Customary Beauty is begotten by the Use of our Senses to those Objects which are usually pleasing to us because of other Causes, a Familiarity of particular inclination breeds Love of Things not in themselves lovely.
—Sir Christopher Wren, Parentalia: Or Memoires of the Family of the Wrens (1750)

The psychic stature of the museum cannot be ignored, least of all by the revisionist architect, who cannot freely move or enlarge any cultural icon. The constraints placed on change are rooted in historical precedent, as we see with the Whitney, the Guggenheim, and the Art Institute in Chicago, or mired deep in the politics of the times or the institution itself—the situation at the Tate in London and the Museum of Modern Art in New York. The successful resolutions of these complex issues at the Art Institute in 1988 and MOMA in 1984 are particularly instructive. They reveal two thoroughly disparate architects—Thomas Beeby, committed to historicism, and Cesar Pelli, a frontline modernist—in the beginning bound by the limitations of their projects yet nudging free at last, despite their divergent methods.

In Chicago's Art Institute, Beeby inherited a museum thoroughly classical and orthodox in origin and practice. From the beginning, indeed, the Art Institute has consistently measured its success both by the number of visitors it attracts and by its adherence to what Chicagoans assumed to be the high European museum model. After a stumbling start as the Chicago Academy of Fine Arts in 1882, the Art Institute outgrew one remodeled mansion home after another until it joined forces with the World's Columbian Exposition to construct a stately Beaux Arts mansion, which first served the fair in 1893 and then became the Institute's permanent home. Designed by the august Boston firm of Shepley, Rutan, and Coolidge, the Art Institute's

Renaissance-inspired building, powerfully centered by rows of columns nested beneath its peaked and pedimented roof, embodied haute cuisine architecture at the end of the last century. Inside, the visitor is carefully led up a grand staircase with galleries arranged around it as suites of rooms, each one illuminated by natural light pouring in through skylights. Perched proudly on its east-west axis, the Art Institute's core building, though amended time and again, had always defied radical tampering—until Beeby added the immense South Building (128,000 square feet). One searches in vain in the history of this institution for ev-

idence of internal dissent on artistic policy or for an architectural challenge to the rational Beaux Arts symmetry of the core. In 1982 when a campaign was announced to raise $67 million for the museum, partly to renovate and refurbish, the funds were quickly supplied by local corporations and donors.

Pelli, on the other hand, found exactly the opposite conditions both within and without MOMA. Having finally won a hard-fought competition with twelve other designers, he then faced a contentious, strong-minded board of trustees, three of whom (Philip Johnson, Gordon Bunshaft, and Ivan Chermayeff) were architects and designers of stature. Pelli was also presented with clear directives about the shape and size of the galleries by depart-

ments whose independence was equally strong. Additionally, Pelli was asked to design a 44-story condominium next door to MOMA for a private developer in order to finance the $55 million expansion. This deal had been arranged when the hard-strapped museum joined forces with the state of New York to create an independent body called the Trust for Cultural Resources. The Trust managed the sale of the air rights over the museum's midtown site to a private developer and issued more than $40 million in tax-exempt bonds for the project. It also acted as yet another strong-willed client. Before Pelli was even hired for the Trust he found a model and plan developed by architect Richard Weinstein showing the exact height and

129

placement of the tower. He also found an aroused press and public focusing on every step taken to revise a building that had become, since its doors first opened in 1939, one of the nerve centers of the city.

In their own ways both Pelli and Beeby were perfectly suited to these challenges. Born in Argentina, sharpened in the give-and-take of high corporate architecture as the head of design for Gruen and Associates in Los Angeles—and newly appointed dean of architecture at Yale—Pelli was "modern" in the classic sense that from start to finish his hard-edged, glass-and-steel architecture epitomized Wren's

130

concept of natural beauty. Beeby, though younger and less experienced than Pelli, was equally devoted to the metaphysics of the museum he was asked to extend. A confirmed postmodern revivalist, he saw a precious beauty in the Beaux-Arts detailing of the core building as well as in its limestone exterior, formidable staircase, and classical axis. Delighted by Skidmore, Owings & Merrill's cleaning and restoration in 1986 of courtyards, crown moldings, neoclassical door frames, gridded skylights, and ornaments in the "old" building, Beeby assiduously repeated these details in the halls and on the walls of his own three-story addition, often insisting on a purity of execution that surpassed the original workmanship. The results tempted him to claim that the new South Building might appear to be older than the core, the quintessence of familiar and comfortable "Customary Beauty," as defined by Wren. Beeby also laid out his galleries on a strictly linear classical plan, using fixed walls and overhead natural lighting in the manner of the beloved picture gallery invented by the German architect Leo von Klenze in the last century. Often, indeed, Beeby publicly proclaimed the superiority of the fixed, symmetrical gallery over the flexible, wide-open "special exhibitions" space invented in the twentieth century.

Yet the grand irony of Beeby's commission was this: the Art Institute asked for and got one of the largest "special exhibition" galleries in the world, Regenstein Hall, which encompasses 19,300 square feet of space. By providing temperature and humidity controls in 14-foot modules on the ceiling of this huge area, Beeby and his colleagues in fact gave the Art Institute an almost infinitely flexible space that can be divided into spaces as large or small as is necessary. In yet another significant gesture to contemporary functional needs Beeby wrapped the "servant" spaces inside his limestone walls around the galleries so that loading docks, carpentry shops, and support services are easily accessible to each gallery and most of all Regenstein Hall, where a stream of temporary exhibitions dictate constant change.

131
Aerial view of the garden facade of the Museum of Modern Art, New York.

132
Hammond Beeby and Babka, Inc. Entrance to the Daniel F. and Ada L. Rice Building through the old South Building of the Art Institute of Chicago.

133
*Hammond Beeby
and Babka, Inc.
Daniel F. and Ada L.
Rice Building,
Art Institute of Chicago.
Gallery installation.*

134
*Hammond Beeby
and Babka, Inc.
Daniel F. and Ada L.
Rice Building,
Art Institute of Chicago.
Interior, Roger McCor-
mick Memorial
Courtyard.*

133

The Art of
PAUL GAUGUIN

THE ROGER McCORMICK MEMORIAL COURT

Of course a stroll through Beeby's South Building reveals none of this ingenuity. In the manner of his predecessors, Shepley, Rutan, and Coolidge, Beeby's grand axes encourage the public to enter the South Building by passing through firmly traditional picture galleries with fixed installations. If the visitor enters on the first floor he or she transits through the sculpture court and around the American collection before reaching Regenstein Hall, a space "totally without character," as the architect often said, changing its face and scale with each new display. Hardly a turn or an ascent in the South Building does not offer a view down yet another axis that terminates with either a primary work of art from the permanent collection or a glimpse of the stately surrounding parks and boulevards. Calm, serene, reposed, the South Building is true to its classical faith—and the intentions of its architect.

The added-on West Wing of the Museum of Modern Art, however, confronts rather than calms the visitor. From the moment of entry into the expanded lobby we immediately face through an immense curtain wall of paneled glass an immense sculpture garden ringed with trees and glimpses of Manhattan's skyscrapers. Gone are the low ceilings and darkened aura of the "old" MOMA, opened in the days when museums often resembled nothing so much as private men's clubs and expected a similar attendance—in the hundreds rather than the tens of thousands. The curtain wall is in fact Pelli's main contribution to this otherwise carefully hedged and controlled expansion. The conscious intention of Pelli's lobby—to attract and delight large crowds with a composition celebrating nature and the world—provides a perfect foil to the Art Institute and to Beeby, who neatly succeeded Pelli as architecture dean at Yale in 1987. In the end, Pelli managed to lead MOMA away from its view of the museum as a club and the galleries within as bourgeois living rooms. Beeby, who occasionally referred to the MOMA lobby as a "supermarket," managed the reverse, purifying the Art Institute's commitment to the gallery as a focus for meditation, hedged about by references to the ennobling (classical) past.

As Beeby cloaked the structural bravura of Regenstein Hall in axis and ornament, Pelli softened the pointed edge of his lobby by preserving after much dispute the original white metal-and-glass gridded facade of 11 West 53rd Street completed in 1939 by Edward Durrell Stone and Philip Goodwin—a facade that supremely embodied Wren's "natural" geometric beauty.

135
*Cesar Pelli
and Associates.
Addition to the
Museum of Modern Art,
New York.
Garden view.*

136
*Museum of Modern Art,
New York.
Interior of old galleries.*

135

136

Though opposed at first by a majority of the trustees, Pelli achieved with this single act both the domestication of the museum's expanded presence on the street and the psychic preservation of the old "Modern." In 1964 Philip Johnson had already added the dark-toned East Wing; with the addition of the West Wing, MOMA virtually doubled the length of its facade. Pelli correctly argued that the destruction of the old Stone-Goodwin grid in favor of one unified facade would be overpowering on the street below. In the end his design for the West Wing adroitly blended Johnson's East Wing with the beloved #11 facade. Repeating the module, scale, and alignment of the Stone-Goodwin building on the facade while elsewhere retaining the dark gray metals and glass of Johnson's addition, the three-part facade blends classic and revisionist modern while avoiding a long, monotonous presence.

The lobby, however, does not compromise with the past. Pelli's decisions here were largely prompted, and defended, on the basis of demographics, program, and circulation. The museum's new, expanded audience, he argued, arrives with a different, considerably upgraded set of expectations. "The old audience was a self-appointed elite," he contended, "with the masses beyond. Now the masses have come to MOMA."[21] Their arrival necessitated an entrance that welcomed rather than excluded; it also meant that circulation had to be eased. Rather than expect-

ing the visitor to find his way through a mazelike series of "rooms," the museum, Pelli argued, has to offer direct access to a variety of programs: the West Wing's 168,000 square feet includes theaters, a photography gallery, video viewing spaces, and architecture and design as well as painting and sculpture galleries.

Pelli's answer was a series of escalators that does in fact recall Macy's (if not Gimbel's). It moves thousands of people a day up and down with a minimum of congestion. At each of the wing's six floors visitors can alight and immediately enter the gallery of their choice without enduring the others. Once "modern" largely in concept and address (its gridded facade), MOMA, in Pelli's hands, has been transformed into a structure paced to the demographic needs of its time, one that embraces a "natural" beauty, rooted in the geometry of ease, motion, and the city beyond. In the new, expanded MOMA, art and life mix, while in Chicago they are kept distinct.

In their subtle, skillful blending of the contradictions inherent in adding, reclaiming, or revising the past and the present of the museum, Beeby and Pelli are anomalies. The revisionist efforts in Chicago and in New York both accept and exploit the ambiguity if not contradiction implicit in history—and the human animal. On the highest level, the museum is itself paradoxical, harboring objects prized by the financial and intellectual elite yet displayed before the voracious public (or "masses," as Pelli put it). The ungainly, asymmetrical Metropolitan Museum as well as the bulging, swarming Los Angeles County Museum of Art, the tightly con-

stricted Des Moines Museum and the suddenly heterodox Tate in London all reflect this tension. Growing, spreading, racing to contain its collection, its public, and its popular attractions, the museum inevitably adopts a multi-form architecture that ignores rules as does spoken language itself—as well as the complex social formulae of postmodern society. Neither speech nor society nor revisionist museum architecture conforms to correct grammar.

Each architect, each director, each funder wants as well to leave his temporal mark on the museum. In the Palazzo Grassi or Chicago's Art Institute the mark of the late twentieth century may simply be the ubiquitous computer terminal or the open spaces in Regenstein Hall. In a masterful melange of interior spaces by Charles Moore for the Williams College Museum of Art in Williamstown, Massachusetts, visitors are explicitly reminded that contradiction reigns supreme when they pass from the central rotunda of a Greek Revival gallery (1846) through each succeeding renovation (including Moore's own mawkish postmodern addition in 1983) into a large, open, loft-style wing at the far end of the museum (1987). Here, as elsewhere, the insistence of each specific time, hand—and, often, benefactor—is persistent and inevitable.

137

137
Cesar Pelli
and Associates.
Addition to the
Museum of Modern Art,
New York.
Garden view from the
northeast.

The Period Style

It will have been noted that the Nuer time dimension is narrow. Valid history ends a century ago, and tradition, generously measured, takes us back only ten to twelve generations in lineage structure. . . . How shallow is Nuer time may be judged from the fact that the tree under which mankind came into being was still standing in Western Nuerland a few years ago!
—*E. E. Evans-Pritchard, The Nuer (1940)*

Though our sense of time has been expanded by research, education, and their dissemination, our convictions about the past are as fallible as the Nuer people of the southern Sudan region of Africa. In this sense the lovingly re-created classicism of Beeby's South Building as well as Pelli's defiantly preserved white grid are the logical equivalents of the original tree still standing in Western Nuerland in the late 1930s. Along with the less skillful revivals that dotted the landscape of architectural fashion in the 1970s and 1980s, the additive Art Institute and re-formed MOMA may one day be perceived as examples of a temporary rather than a permanent attitude toward museum growth. I raise this point because historical logic demands us to consider the possibility that this chapter studies what might become a period style. Consider this: as art and society continue their relentless march away from the practical conditions imposed on planning and construction in the distant, romanticized, classical period—and away from the heroic optimism of the early moderns—the past may no longer be seen as an infallible model for additive growth. The revisions of the future, in brief, might well move toward the future.

138
*Cesar Pelli
and Associates.
Addition to the
Museum of Modern Art,
New York.
Interior with escalator.*

The Roy and Niuta Titus Theaters

Chapter Five THE ANTIMUSEUM: ALTERNATIVES

139
Walter De Maria.
The Lightning Field.
Quemodo, New
Mexico.

The objects that are put in the showcases of our museums are sanctified. . . . They are pronounced beautiful and held up as models, and thus is established that fatal chain of ideas and their consequences.
—Le Corbusier, "Other Icons: The Museums," in The Decorative Art of Today (1925)

The first problem is to establish the museum as a center for the enjoyment, not the internment, of art. In this project the barrier between the work of art and the community is erased. . . .
—Mies van der Rohe, "Museum for a Small City" (1942)

Monsieur Manet has never wished to protest. On the contrary, the protest, which he never expected, has been directed against himself; this is because those who have been brought up in these [traditional] principles will admit no others. . . .
—Edouard Manet, preface to catalog for his self-organized exhibition, Paris (1867)

I didn't make critical judgments. . . . Nobody ever showed us their work beforehand. I refused to look at slides.
—Jeffrey Lew, Director, 112 Greene Street Workshop, interview (1979)

From their beginnings, dominant state-supported museums like the Louvre or the National Gallery in London have generated political and esthetic opposition that inevitably expressed itself in architectural terms. Though we have no records of any early objections to Ptolemy I's *Mouseion* in ancient Alexandria or Pope Sixtus IV's Museo Capitolino, we can begin to track an anti-museum temper as early as the seventeenth century, when artists in Rome, Paris, and London began to defy official exhibitions or patronage by setting up alternative galleries or inviting the public into their own studios. It is now virtually forgotten that the august Royal Academy of Arts in London was founded in 1768 by Sir Joshua Reynolds and other painters as an act of protest against the court, the National Gallery, and the quasi-official Incorporated Society of Artists. The decision by the French revolutionaries to supplant the royal Luxembourg Gallery with a public space in the Louvre was itself an anti-establishment gesture as were the ferocious protests by artists against the Louvre's installation and the organizational policies that followed.

Throughout the nineteenth century artists and public alike continued to defy the dictates of official culture, particularly in France. Time and again the infamous salon exhibitions, controlled by a small circle of academic painters and government officials, generated protest in the form of the Salon des Refusés. Filled with the paintings and drawings of rejected, anti-academic artists and installed in a variety

140

141

140
*Aerial view of original
factory site of the future
Massachusetts Museum
of Contemporary Art,
North Adams,
Massachusetts.*

141
*Original factory site
of the future
Massachusetts Museum
of Contemporary Art,
North Adams,
Massachusetts.*

of gallery spaces, this unofficial event later generated independent power and prestige, particularly when the impudent young Impressionists took it over in 1873. The Impressionists also fine-tuned the genre of the self-curated one-person "alternative" exhibition. In 1867, for instance, Manet opened his own one-man display and published his own catalog written in his own words. In 1874 the cream of the Impressionist painters rented the spacious studio owned by the illustrious photographer Nadar for a group show that included Manet, Cézanne, Degas, Monet, and Renoir, an event now certified in every art history textbook.

Inspired by these events, Félix Fénéon, Georges Seurat, Paul Signac, and Odilon Redon organized in 1884 the Société des Artistes Indépendants "for the suppression of juries and . . . to help artists to freely present their work." Throughout the century, artists like Gustave Moreau in France, Antonio Canova in Italy, and J.M.W. Turner in England took aggressive steps to protect their work from absorption into the enormous black holes that the great museums had become. Canova stipulated that his works be hung together in a studio devoted solely to that purpose as did Moreau. The latter, who explicitly used the term "museum," in his will, may be the first man to become the posthumous director of his own museum, which exists in Paris to this day. Turner also wrote several detailed, impassioned wills leaving his paintings to the National Gallery, stipulating exactly where and how they should be installed and demanding a "Turner's Gallery."[22]

In this century the loyal opposition has been further fired by the religiosity inherent in the growing reverence for "art" in all its forms, as well as the proliferation of museums. During and immediately after World War I the Dada painters, poets, and performers thrived on opposition to the status quo as exemplified by the museum. Though William Rubin is correct to point out that often Dada produced works of exquisite formal interest thereby widening and enriching the province of the fine arts—Duchamp's "found" bottle rack, for

example—the raging antipathy that underscored all its works cannot be ignored. By painting a moustache on the *Mona Lisa*, by signing and displaying an ordinary urinal at the Exhibition of Independent Painters in New York in 1917, and by publicly disavowing the practice of painting, Marcel Duchamp made this undercurrent explicit.

In one form or another, with one sort of nuance or another, the anti-art/antimuseum current has thrived in this century, sometimes explicitly—as in the case of the Italian artist Piero Manzoni, whose elegant metal container of excrement, *Merde d'Arte* (1961),[23] is a direct descendant of the urinal—but more often implicitly as we can see with the intentionally casual, open "alternative spaces"[24] that flourished throughout the West in the 1960s and 1970s, most of all in the United States. As a signal progenitor of the antimuseum critique, Dada was proud of its birth in a cabaret in Zurich in 1915. Nearly all of the early Dada exhibitions and performances were deliberately staged under rough circumstances—in beer halls, factories, and parks. Later the younger artists, curators, and certain irreverent collectors in New York, London, and Cologne favored abandoned industrial lofts, schools, and even virtually inaccessible ranch lands, mountains, and stretches of desert (Walter De Maria's *Lightning Field*, for example, is an activist work of metal-rod sculpture mounted in the New Mexico desert). In almost all of these cases—those where actual interior spaces were involved, that is—the architect/curator was committed to a neutrality so intense that it began to border on a studied style. In stripped-down spaces like P.S.1, a freewheeling center of contemporary art located in Long Island City near Manhattan, the work of art reigns theoretically supreme, presented against the backdrop of a peeling, abandoned schoolhouse, with no evidence of the architect's hand or mind.

Beginning with Le Corbusier's strident antimuseum essays and manifestos, certain professional architects have struggled to develop new ways to exhibit art. With a few exceptions, however, architects have preferred to reform the conventional container rather than remove it. Between the

lines of his harsh assault on the museum's exclusivity and its inevitable prejudice in favor of objects collected by the wealthy, Corbusier proposes a new and complex architectonic form that would allow the museum to display everyday objects beside anointed works of painting and sculpture. Corbu's vision is best embodied in the endless sprawl of abandoned factories purchased in 1989 by the fledgling Museum of Contemporary Art in North Adams, Massachusetts—a museum in which any product of art or life can be philosophically accommodated. Mies van der Rohe's earlier determination to avoid the dark confining atmosphere of the overdesigned museum led to the creation of the pristine glass box that is West Berlin's New National Gallery, a building universally admired as architecture and condemned as an exhibition space, since the intensity of light requires the erection of clumsy partitions.

Some architects have studiously avoided the imperial museum's conventional apostrophe to itself or to classical precedent—among them Peter Eisenman, in his Wexner Center for the Visual Arts in Columbus, Ohio (see Chapter VI) and his proposal for the art gallery at the University of California at Long Beach; Jean-Paul Carlhian in a pair of cavernous underground museums in the midst of Washington, D.C.'s Smithsonian Institution (designed under the auspices of Shepley, Bulfinch, Richardson, and Abbot of Boston); and José Rafael Moneo, in his Museum of Roman Art in Mérida. Each in their own way has avoided traditional museum design strategies, in some cases with explicitly radical departures, as at Ohio State, and in others more subtly (Carlhian's museums, buried in the earth, still maintain classical references). What we began to see toward the end of the century was the rise of the museum as a form to address specific issues of landscape, topology, history, and site as well as general issues of the past and academic art history. At this point, perhaps, the museum began to depart in the highest sense from itself.

Once inside the museum [art is] divorced from context, from any context save a hushed didactic strenuousness. It becomes good for no one. For whom? For anyone. . . . No art where you use your mind; dead art where the sign says ART.
—Hugh Kenner, "Epilogue: The Dead-Letter Office," in Museums in Crisis (1971)

The sixties was the first time since the Renaissance that artists found their own space, when artists no longer were confined to the private space of the collector.
—Giuseppe Panza di Biumo, interview (1988)

The bombardment of the museums with more art than they can rationally order or present is the crisis of our time for those who collect art in order to defend and promote its message. The big museum with massive attendance is no longer desirable for many of us. With the personal, single-focus museum you can begin to humanize art, to bring it down to human scale.
—Henry Hopkins, Director of the Weisman Collection, interview (1988)

Certainly it was the expansion of the museum that fed the antimuseum in the decades that followed World War II. The countless alternative spaces opened by small groups of artists and collectors in great urban centers during these years were inspired not only by the desire to exhibit work that might otherwise go unseen, in the manner of Reynolds and Manet, but the urge as well to de-estheticize art, to free it from the suffocating envelope of grand, traditional culture. When in 1969 collectors Holly and Howard Solomon opened a ground-floor loft space in Soho, then the warehouse district of New York, they deliberately eschewed any form of control over what the artists they selected might do in the space. This hands-off policy was summed up by the gallery's totally neutral site name, 98 Greene Street. Not far away, artist Jeffrey Lew founded an even larger and looser space, the 112 Greene Street Workshop. Here Lew rejected a policy of critical exclusion so rigorously that artists often began to build or perform without his knowledge. Both of these influential Greene Street spaces exuded a raw industrial vitality that grew from their surly unfinished surroundings as well as the dominance of the minimalist style of the early seventies, which emphasized—particularly in sculpture—massive scale, minimal forms, and unprocessed industrial materials. Gordon Matta-Clark's *Dumpster* (1972), a huge, refuse-filled dumpster truck that bridged the street space between 98 and 112 Greene, perfectly summed up the mood, as did

An-Architecture, the exhibition he later assembled of raw anonymous photographs selected by his colleagues, each one depicting extraordinary studios, rooms, and buildings untouched by an architect's hand.

Completing the cycle launched on Greene Street, an immense, completely recycled "alternative space" named "P.S.1" opened on June 9, 1976, in an abandoned public school building in Long Island City, in the borough of Queens adjacent to Manhattan. The first exhibition, entitled simply *Rooms*, clearly defined its unorthodox attitude. In each of the seventy-eight vacated "classrooms" neither the artist nor the curator nor the architect made the slightest attempt to neutralize the space. Instead, the peeling walls, blackboards, and stained floorboards were often foregrounded rather than hidden. In this desanctified context the work of art radiated a new set of meanings, particularly its opposition to what was regarded as the bourgeois gentrification of official culture. This attitude was vividly expressed again by Matta-Clark in *Doors, Floors, Doors*. Here the simple act of removing a series of basement doors permitted the visitor a long, focused view of a subterranean landscape stretching out through buried and forgotten rooms.

At P.S.1, the profile of the restoration architect—Shael Shapiro—became that of an invisible man. Though he deftly chopped down partitions, painted walls, and shored up staircases, Shapiro's work was hardly noticed and largely ignored by the world at large. Indeed, the key architectural decision here was simply the decision by P.S.1's parent organization, the Institute of Art and Urban Resources, Inc., to locate in this immense, abandoned Romanesque revival building. The widely imitated rusticity of P.S.1's architectural and programming style springs almost entirely from its vital "found" container.

142

142
Gordon Matta-Clark.
The Dumpster, *1972.*
Wood, doors,
industrial container,
7 × 8 × 20' long.
Daniel Varenne,
Geneva.

143
P.S.1,
Long Island City,
New York.
Exterior.

144
P.S.1,
Long Island City,
New York.
Exterior.

143

144

145

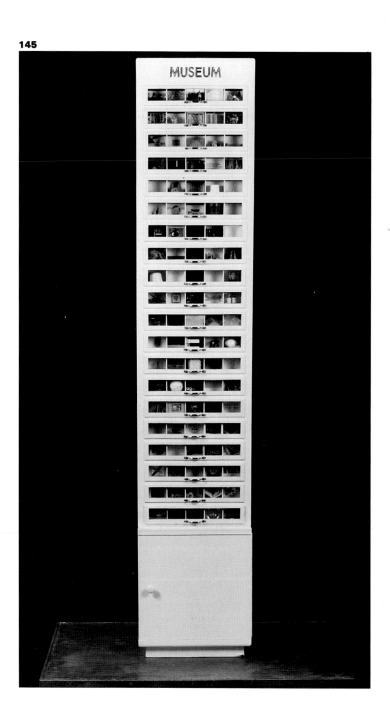

Herbert Distel.
The Museum of
Drawers, 1972.
Mixed media.
Kunsthaus Zurich,
Zurich.

The old school's hundreds of thousands of square feet allowed P.S.1 to commit as much space to the creation of new art by providing open studios as to merely exhibiting it. (Curator-artist-critic Alanna Heiss, an American who had lived and worked extensively in London in the sixties and founded the original Institute of Art and Urban Resources in fact preferred the term "Experimental Workspace" to "gallery" or "museum.") But inevitably the means required to keep P.S.1 alive as well as its own success led it to embrace the larger culture. In the eighties, the Institute's list of benefactors and trustees began to resemble the boards of major museums everywhere, including large corporations as well as state and federal agencies. Meanwhile, its exhibitions expanded beyond the dramatically truncated rooms that housed street-theater performances to include orthodox genres of painting and sculpture curated by museum personnel.

In the ascension of P.S.1 to a loftier status, we are witnessing the genius of co-optive democratic culture, which constantly stretches its boundaries to permit critical agents something of a permanent presence. The non-style of the alternative space rapidly became an official unofficial style, repeated over and over. The peeling wall and warped Corinthian column turned into symbols, no more, no less, of paraconventional esthetic dissent. Patterned on the light-industrial lofts in which many artists began to work in the 1960s and 1970s—as their industrial owners deserted for suburbia—the stark, high-ceilinged skylit gallery is a recurring motif in the work of architects such as Frank Gehry. His Temporary Contemporary in Los Angeles is a direct scion of P.S.1, as is the final gallery at the end of Cesar Pelli's revisionist maze of bourgeois living-room

spaces on the second floor at the Museum of Modern Art, with its raw, gleaming floorboards, fourteen-foot-high ceiling, and streams of bright daylight. Max Gordon's white, clean-limbed renovation in 1985 of 98-A Boundary Road, the huge abandoned factory in London that now houses the elite collection of Doris and Max Saatchi, is similar in origin, as are the bright capacious galleries and deliberately humble clapboard exterior of Renzo Piano's Menil Collection in Houston, which fits as snugly into its lower-middle-class neighborhood as P.S.1 does in the midst of working-class Long Island City.

The conversion of wealthy collectors like the Menils and the Saatchis to the non-style was a critical step. In 1974 Philippa de Menil, daughter of Dominique, who commissioned Piano's Houston masterpiece, founded the Dia Foundation in New York with German art dealer Heiner Friedrich. Both were concerned that the ambitious artists they collected—Joseph Beuys, Walter De Maria, Dan Flavin, Donald Judd—were singularly unsuited to the homogeneous context of most museums, where huge complex installations either don't fit or are quickly disassembled. Menil and Friedrich began to buy up large warehouses and tracts of open land. Precisely as the artists ordered, they placed enormous works of environmental sculpture like De Maria's *Broken Kilometer* (five hundred highly polished brass rods stretching 125 feet) and the *New York Earth Room* (a 3,600-square-foot collection of earth weighing almost 280,000 pounds) inside stripped-down loft spaces renovated by architect Richard Gluckman. De Maria's notorious *Lighting Field*; the neon-tube environments of Dan Flavin, glowing away in an abandoned Long Island firehouse; the rugged, impassive metal sculpture of Donald Judd, sprawled around the site of an old 300-acre army base in Marfa, Texas—these works and many others were purchased and placed on indefinite exhibition, though often days, even weeks pass without a single visitor.

By perpetually exhibiting and preserving works characterized by unconventional materials and scale the Dia Foundation performed in the 1970s and 1980s a critical and largely ignored museum function. When the collapse of oil prices led to a restructuring of the Foundation in 1985 (the Menil family fortune is

146

146
Donald Judd sculpture at the Chinati Foundation, a series of exhibition spaces located primarily on an abandoned military base in Marfa, Texas, and renovated by Judd.

147
Chinati Foundation, Marfa, Texas. Interior with Judd sculpture.

147

148
*Dia Foundation
Gallery,
548 West 22nd Street,
New York.
Exterior.*

149
*Dia Foundation
Gallery,
548 West 22nd Street,
New York.
Interior with installa-
tion of Imi Knoebel
sculptures.*

150
*Dia Foundation
Gallery,
548 West 22nd Street,
New York.
Interior.*

148

closely tied to oil), a group of new directors and curators at Dia began to ease the monolithic policy of continuous display. The Foundation's brand-new four-story warehouse space at 548 West 22nd Street in Manhattan, renovated in 1987 by Gluckman, reveals a last trace of the architect's hand in the non-style. Here a certain level of architectural and artistic variety is sustained by the decision to devote each 9,200-square-foot floor to a different artist each year and by annually revising the floors in keeping with the new artist's needs. But there are also signs of an attempt to endow the floors with a semblance of new identity independent from the artists. Though the load-bearing columns were left untouched and the rows of gridded overhead lights exactly replicated the rhythms imposed by the rows of bays above, Gluckman subtly introduced his presence in minor details of form and tone. On the very top floor the industrial skeleton is entirely absorbed in the newly molded curve of the walls and the bright light admitted by a skylight. Here the rigorous, pure warehouse mood first asserted at Greene Street and P.S.1 begins to soften; architecture begins to appear as an independent agent—that is, in its traditional museum role of embellishment and decoration.

It is hardly an accident that the non-style style flourished at the two extremes of museum management—in low-cost, artist-managed alternative spaces and in gilded institutions created and managed by a single collector, like the Dia Foundation or 98-A Boundary Road in London. Owned and operated by Charles Saatchi, a wealthy British media magnate, and his wife, Doris, a widely published critic, 98-A Boundary Road presents one of the most polemic, single-minded collections of our time, rivaled only by Panza di Biumo's in Italy. Committed to the cosmopolitan, cutting-edge art of the 1970s and 1980s, in both its severe minimalist and florid neo-expressionist phases, the Saatchis purchased a warehouse in a modest middle-class London neighborhood and entrusted its conversion into an exhibition space to Max Gordon. What Gordon wrought there

is a refinement of the warehouse esthetic. 98-A Boundary Road (its official name; the term "museum" is studiously avoided) is a long, low, one-story, gray shed-roofed building that pretends to anonymity in a neighborhood of tiny homes and shops. Once a paint factory, on entrance it presents itself now as a single white-walled, gray cement-floored, straitjacketed space contoured into six smaller spaces. Never does a chair, a bench, a column, or even, with minor exceptions, a wall text relieve or divert the eye; 98-A Boundary Road is the Zen monastery of art watching.

In this cool hushed environment, where the works on display directly reflect the singular, focused intelligence of their owners (the Saatchis collect only a handful of artists), the viewer is clearly expected to focus on the object itself, divorced from any contact with the outside world. Except for the stainless steel grid work under the pitched roofs, Gordon has relentlessly chipped away all of the distractions of the factory he inherited. Wrapped in the folds of this spare esthetic, viewers at 98-A Boundary Road can be forgiven if they deduce—as their hosts surely intend—that Art is its own perfectly constructed end. And, further, that they avoid breathing, if possible: exhaling might break the silence.

Of course Gordon's hand at 98-A Boundary is prominent as he pushes the esthetic of absence to extreme ends. But the proliferation of the personal art museum space has tended to relegate architecture and the architect into a distinctly subsidiary role. Often the polemical goal is primary, as in the case of the Saatchis, of Daniel Terra, who opened a museum in his own name in Chicago in 1988 to house his Impressionism-rich collection, and of Wilhelmina and Wallace Holladay, whose feminist-oriented cache of painting and sculpture became the National Museum of Women in the Arts in Washington, D.C., in 1987. In an era when it became common to acquire art in quantities far beyond the display capacity of a single home or apartment, these collections were formed by men and women who rightly feared that

151
Max Gordon Associates.
Saatchi Museum,
London.
Gallery installation.

152
Max Gordon Associates.
Saatchi Museum,
London.
Gallery installation.

151

152

153

the sharp edge of their works might be blunted in the hands of established museums already laden with a mélange of treasures. Often they commissioned their own Boundary Roads, instructing architects to provide containers hidden behind their contents. In the case of a prolific but careful collector like Frederick Weisman of Los Angeles, whose vast array of avant-garde painting, sculpture, film, and video-tape required large storage spaces, an archive, and a curatorial staff, the decision to establish an exhibition space dictated the appointment of a professional museologist. Henry Hopkins, the respected former director of the San Francisco Museum of Modern Art, was originally charged with the task of finding, negotiating for, and designing a building that would be inevitably controversial, considering the modernity of the collection.

On the grounds of scale alone, the needs of collectors like Weisman, Menil, and particularly Giuseppe Panza di Biumo of Milan demand the subservience of the architecture to a massively functional task that often requires the spartan reconditioning of industrial-age buildings rather than the creation of orthodox museum spaces. When Panza reached the limits of the space available in his eighteenth-century castle in Varese, near Milan, where even the closets were hollowed out to permit the display of art, the Italian collector attempted unsuccessfully to persuade museum after museum to properly install and preserve his huge works of environmental sculpture, which he offered on sixty-year loans. Frustrated, he turned to long-term loan exhibitions mounted by massive institutions like the epic converted hospital in Madrid that is Reina Sofia in Madrid, a converted hospital, and the twenty-eight vacated factories in the aging mill town of North Adams, Massachusetts, which will become the Massachusetts Museum of Contemporary Art. Passionately committed to art that acts beyond the podium or the gallery wall, Panza required almost 300,000 square feet of space to exhibit his collection of works by artists such as Donald Judd, Bruce Nauman, and Richard Serra. One thorough display of work by an ambitious sculptor like Serra might be possible only in the lofts—like those in North Adams—that once contained precisely the forms and materials exploited by the artist.

Panza's refusal to commit his collection to unsuitable spaces parallels the concerns of artists like Moreau and Turner in the last century, who pioneered the formation of museums and galleries devoted entirely to themselves. Isamu Noguchi's

Garden Museum, opened in 1985 not far from the doors of P.S.1 in Long Island City, is the latest determined effort to rebuff the impersonal sepulcher. Frustrated by the curators who preferred certain parts of his work and ignored others, Noguchi decided to buy, design, and equip his own resting place, in effect. "I wanted some protection for the future, that is, when I'm no longer here," he explained. "I tried to get the Whitney, the Metropolitan, and the Museum of Modern Art to help. They couldn't see their way, so I tried to help myself."[25] On the outside his museum,

154
Gallery installation at the Reina Sofia Art Center, Madrid, showing Bruce Nauman's Triangle Room.

155
Courtyard of the Reina Sofia Art Center, Madrid, showing Henry Moore sculpture.

planned in collaboration with Japanese-American architect Shoji Sadao, is as nakedly honest as 112 Greene Street. Noguchi and Sadao wrapped the core of an old redbrick factory in a sharply angled concrete block skin, devoid of decoration, grace, or wit. Inside, however, Noguchi composed a network of twelve quiet, high-ceilinged rooms that open in the Japanese manner onto an interior garden open to the sky. The galleries are filled with works from every period of his life, and Noguchi was hardly self-effacing about what he had done. "I define the reason for the Isamu Noguchi Museum as a desire to show the totality of my work," he said, on the wall of the foyer. With this gesture he had gone beyond even the intrepid acts of Moreau, Turner, or Tadanori Yokoo, who hired the formidable Arata Isozaki to fulfill his dream of perfect presentation. Given the museum's task of sorting out and dividing the fine from the mundane, Noguchi's self-designed, self-financed, and self-managed museum becomes the ultimate act of self-definition.

155

156
*Isamu Noguchi
and Shoji Sadao.
Isamu Noguchi Garden
Museum,
Long Island City,
New York.
View of garden.*

157
*Isamu Noguchi
and Shoji Sadao.
Isamu Noguchi Garden
Museum,
Long Island City,
New York.
Gallery installation.*

158
*Isamu Noguchi
and Shoji Sadao.
Isamu Noguchi Garden
Museum,
Long Island City,
New York.
Gallery installation.*

156

157

158

The Museum as Site, If Not Place

Unlike the other museums where the buildings are monuments, our building acts as a background, as a platform for environmental art, nature, and history.
—*Peter Eisenman, press release from the University Art Museum, California State University, Long Beach (1987)*

I never had any doubts about going underground. My architect said "You go down to hell," but later he agreed that we could make a heaven under the earth here.
—*S. Dillon Ripley, interview (1987)*

The impatience with conventional museum design that has characterized much late twentieth-century architecture takes many more forms than antistyle. José Rafael Moneo's National Museum of Roman Art in Mérida, Spain (1985), for instance, is a studied rebuff to the overdecorated colossus as well as the neutral container. Located on the site of an ancient Roman ruin, Moneo's structure, meant to collect and exhibit Roman artifacts, turns both history and content into form. The museum's exterior evokes the solemnity and regularity of the Roman brick wall, its segments laid in delicate formal rows. Within, Moneo has organized the museum by means of parallel brick walls crossed with grand arches. Above, through large, distinctly modern skylights, the sun beams directly into the galleries, illuminating richly detailed brickwork that recalls the past—and Piranesi's macabre drawings.

Moneo's double-coded use of the museum-of-artifacts as artifact itself was paralleled during the mid-eighties by the American team of Peter Eisenman and Jacquelin Robertson—first in their reconstruction of a destroyed armory into the Wexner Center for the Visual Arts at Ohio State University in Columbus, Ohio (see Chapter VI), and second in their proposed art gallery for the University of California at Long Beach (1986). The plan for the Long Beach structure in fact seems to eschew both the denotative and connotative dimensions of the "art museum" it is supposed to house. Here the 23-acre museum

159
José Rafael Moneo.
Museum of Roman Art,
Mérida, Spain.

160
Eisenman Robertson
Architects, and Hugh
Gibbs & Donald Gibbs
Architects.
University Art Museum,
California State Uni-
versity, Long Beach.
Site plan.

161
Eisenman Robertson
Architects, and Hugh
Gibbs & Donald Gibbs
Architects.
University Art Museum,
California State Uni-
versity, Long Beach.
Model.

160

161

complex speaks of ecological, industrial, and political history, turning itself into nothing less than a layered representation of the region's past. The central building is cut along the major geographic fault line of the area, which separates the deeply buried North American and Pacific plates. Placed around it are historical artifacts that have either been renovated or completely re-created. These include a resurrected nineteenth-century Greene and Greene house, an oil derrick that recalls the once-thriving industry that powered Long Beach in the past, a golden pond representing the California gold rush in 1849, and a pier recovered from an almost-forgotten Long Beach sea coast resort that thrived in the twenties. Rather than comment upon itself, the Eisenman-Robertson museum at Long Beach dares to speak of historical issues based in the broader site and city it inhabits, transforming itself into a form of historical documentation rather than a mere treasure house.

On a far larger and blunter scale, the paired Smithsonian Institution galleries devoted to African and Asian art, opened in Washington, D.C., in 1987, confront a similar issue. Driven directly into the earth by architect Jean-Paul Carlhian and blessed by the Institution's mercurial director, S. Dillon Ripley, they have created a new kind of cultural fault line. Presented with a plot of land on the Smithsonian Quadrangle in the middle of Washington, D.C., ringed with an eclectic mélange of revered old buildings (including the neo-Gothic Smithsonian "castle" by James Renwick), first Ripley and then

Carlhian decided that the site's problems could only be solved with a layered set of underground galleries hidden beneath a formal garden. Trained in the Beaux-Arts tradition, Carlhian provides visitors with two small entrance pavilions shaped as a dome and a pyramid, pavilions that echo nearby motifs and open into a sequential series of formal spaces leading down into the ground. We descend a majestic winding stairway beneath brilliant glass domes that were originals intended to open up the earth to the sky above. But the 90-foot-long gallery on the second central level roofed with skylights quickly incurred the wrath of the curatorial staffs of the Arthur M. Sackler Gallery of Asian Art and the National Museum of African Art. They chopped Carlhian's broad, expansive space into a series of small labyrinthine galleries and boarded up the skylights. The grand vision of an inner earth linked to the heavens above that inspired Carlhian's design had set his otherwise perfectly traditional structure distinctly apart from its colleagues—here, the museum-as-site had almost completely divorced itself from its role as treasure house. But that vision was finally forced to give way to the demands of the curatorial profession, forever grounded in the requirements of installation and display.

162
*Smithsonian
Institution,
Washington, D.C.
The original "castle"
building is situated in
the middle between the
more recent Arthur M.
Sackler Gallery on the
left and the National
Museum of African Art
on the right.
Drawing.*

163
*Shepley, Bulfinch,
Richardson, and
Abbott.
National Museum
of African Art,
Smithsonian Institution,
Washington, D.C.*

164
*Shepley, Bulfinch,
Richardson, and
Abbott.
Arthur M. Sackler
Gallery,
Smithsonian Institution,
Washington, D.C.
Stairway.*

165
*Shepley, Bulfinch,
Richardson, and
Abbott.
Arthur M. Sackler
Gallery,
Smithsonian Institution,
Washington, D.C.*

164

165

The Museum as Object beyond the Object

The dispute that wrecked Jean-Paul Carlhian's vision of the underground Smithsonian sums up the dilemma posed by any attempt to impose innovative contextual or structural meaning on a genre of architecture that resists anything other than homage to itself—that is, to the treasure house or to museological tradition. Ironically, the means of freeing both the museum and architecture from this treasure, from the mass of collected objects, appeared only at the end of a century when historical revivalism thrived. Corbusier had dreamed of an "endless" museum stocked with everything of value, one that refused to defer to country-house taste. Late in his life Duchamp, who once said that he could fit his lifework into a suitcase,[26] illustrated his thesis by compiling a tiny *boite-en-valise* ("portable box") complete with photographs, folding stool, miniature urinal, and a vial of "Paris air." Duchamp's act was echoed by a more neutral curator, the Swiss critic and collector Herbert Distel, who dutifully prepared a six-foot-high *Museum of Drawers* for exhibition in 1972. Each drawer, treated as a separate "gallery," was stocked with tiny drawings, objects, and paintings by an international cadre of five hundred artists ranging from Andy Warhol to Walasse Ting.[27]

But the perfection of electronic and mechanical reproduction has converted the once-radical propositions of Duchamp, Distel, and others into tame prophecies and directly challenges the pretensions of architecture to contemporaneity of any

sort. With rare exceptions, museums that announce their intention to house and program uniquely modern art forms like film or videotape contradict their innovative spirit in their architectural housing. Though the Museum of Broadcasting in New York City boasted proudly that its new building on 52nd Street would house two theaters, eighty-five television monitors, and twenty-five radio consoles to allow practically total access to its collection, none of its officials blanched when at a packed press conference architect Philip Johnson rightly compared the peaked cornice, limestone facing, and two-story arch of the model to the medieval church. "Museums have taken the place of churches in our culture,"[28] he declared in a statement released by the museum. When the American Museum of the Moving Image opened in the same city in the fall of 1988, it was concisely housed by Gwathmey Siegel within the remains of a precious industrial-age landmark, a beautiful reinforced-concrete factory equipped with all the icons associated with the alternative spaces of yore—exposed columns, girders and beams, and expansive windows. Not even Gwathmey Siegel's glass-enclosed stair tower, a striking element of the facade, nor the abundant theaters for film and video could defuse the metaphorical reference to another time, mode, and attitude.

In their proposal for California's Ansel Adams Center for the Friends of Photography, in 1986, SITE, a free-spirited group of American architects, for once attempted

166

166
Gwathmey Siegel
& Associates.
American Museum of
the Moving Image,
New York.
Detail of exterior.

167
John Burgee Architects.
Museum of
Broadcasting,
New York.
Drawing of exterior.

a modest link between the visual information presented by the museum and its very
contemporary content. Because the construction of a camera's interior and shutter
mechanism suggests a building enclosure,
SITE offered in effect an enclosed "dark-
room" by covering a glass structure with
sod and confronting the entering visitor
with aperturelike arches at the entrance.
But by and large contemporary architecture has remained deaf, mute, and blind
when it comes to openly representing or
suggesting the contents of a museum
committed to the art of mechanical
reproduction.

In a compelling essay entitled "The
Demand for a Contemporary Language of
Architecture," Christian Norberg-Schulz
argues that those he calls "late Modern"
architects have run out of a signifying
language—that is, a contemporary form to
express the needs of contemporary life.
While he expresses sympathy for the postmodern attraction to the symbolic and
meaning-laden architecture of the past,
particularly classicism, Norberg-Schulz
also argues that the functional implications
of any architectural element, whether door,
stairway, or gallery, demands a simple,
one-to-one functional relationship that bor-
ders on archetype—"the revelation," he
says, "of hidden relationships."[29] What
this implies is that the fully contemporary
museum, the purest of antimuseums, must
closely stitch together program, that is
content, and architecture, or form. If the
Museum of Broadcasting and the American
Museum of the Moving Image contradict
their content, so do their programs, which
are based largely upon the collection and
preservation of objects from the past.
Mies van der Rohe's idealistic vision of a
"Museum for a Small City," planned and
sketched in 1942, was conceived as a
transparent cube primarily for the display
of Picasso's *Guernica*, and later came to
life in magnified form as Berlin's New
National Gallery. But in reality the heavy
traditional exhibitions mounted by those
who took over the day-to-day life of the
museum fell out of step with Mies's wide-
open, flexible space.

168

169

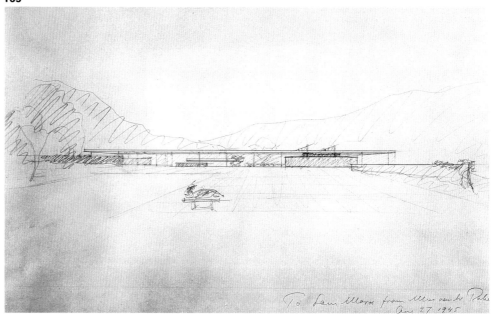

168
SITE Projects, Inc.
Ansel Adams Friends
of Photography Center,
San Francisco,
California.
Model.

169
Ludwig Mies van
der Rohe.
Project: Museum for
a Small City, *1942.*
Drawing,
whereabouts unknown.
Courtesy, Mies van
der Rohe Archive,
Museum of Modern Art,
New York.

*The Unknown Museum
has no snack bar,
checkroom, lavatories,
bookstore, wings, addi-
tions, or annexes . . . a
sense of deep history
pervades . . . even
though nothing in the
collection is truly
antique. The rapid
deterioration of mass-
produced materials
suggests an accumula-
tion of centuries rather
than decades. . . .
It is a shrine to the
phenomenon of mass
production. . . .*
—Philip Garner, "The
Unknown Museum,"
(1985)

*. . . Architecture may
perhaps be summed up
in this strange faculty
of the most beautiful
architectural works to
offer the image of a si-
lent necessity, timeless
and universal.*
—Bernard Huet, "After
the Glorification of
Reason" (1988)

In his classic polemic, "The Age of Mechanical Reproduction," Walter Benjamin had argued passionately in 1936 that the creation of the means to reproduce images exactly would steadily reduce what he called the "aura" of the art object. Later, Philip Garner contended that the glut of mass production itself would transform—if not eliminate—the fine art object. Of course none of these prophecies—like Mies's, which implies a totally transparent architectural language—were realized in the century in which they were proclaimed.[30] If anything, as we will see in the Afterword, "original" works of art escalated in value and desirability as never before, prompted rather than restrained by widespread dissemination in books and magazines. But certainly Benjamin, André Malraux (in his classic text *The Museum Without Walls*), William Ivins, and others were correct to detect within the realm of mechanical reproduction an expanding arena of creativity if not collecting. With the onset of film and especially television, this arena becomes almost post-architectural in the sense that these defin-

itively contemporary media act beyond the museological sphere, most often in the private space of the home if not the mind of the viewer who beholds them.

For this reason, it seems fair to declare the unofficial non-style first realized in the raw lofts and factories converted by artists and architects in the 1970s to be the final summit—in our time—of the increasingly official antimuseum. Even later, in the precocious distillation of this working-class ideal at 98-A Boundary Road and in the large, vacant installations mounted by the Dia Foundation, we find compelling primeval references largely absent from formal museum architecture. By its recall of a historic industrial order, the abandoned factory, school, or field reminds us of the origins of art itself, at once in the ancestral caves of our past and in the perpetually renewed mind of the child.

Chapter Six   **THE MUSEUM IN THE NEXT CENTURY**

170
Bernard Tschumi
Associates.
Parc de la Villette,
Paris.
Folie P6.

We must keep on hoping that with every project the architect is building toward a better future. This is the sense of progress that, notwithstanding the weaknesses, deviations, and shortcomings of our work, I call Gallilean: experiri plavet (to experience is pleasing). . . .
—Aldo Rossi in Aldo Rossi: Buildings and Projects *(1985)*

The last century is still so close to us and we are so busy keeping up with the present one that it is hard for us to keep up with the meaning of the fact that the last hundred and fifty years have seen the greatest and most thoroughgoing revolution in technology and science that has ever taken place in so short a time.
—William Ivins, Jr., Prints and Visual Communication *(1953)*

The Center [should] be dedicated to experimentation and vanguard artistic activity. . . . It will include activity in the visual arts not only in studio art but in the disciplines of architecture . . . computer graphics, electronic music and art, photography, cinema, landscape architecture, music, dance, and theater.
—Program of requirements, Wexner Center for the Visual Arts, Ohio State University *(1985)*

Given the overpowering presence of past and present models, it is by no means certain that the museum of the next century will differ sharply from its predecessor. Once constructed, massive works of architecture like ancient cathedrals and temples are rarely replaced. They continue to serve their original function long past the point at which the function itself may be essential. The purpose of the museum has been extended and revised in this century under the pressure of expanding demand, but there is no guarantee that it will continue indefinitely.

Yet the next century deserves a new museum, for certainly the conditions that obtained at the birth of the old will no longer exist. The divide between high and low, between ownership and free access to "art," between the objects or activities permitted to aspire to the realm of art is steadily closing. Though the aura of originality attached to the sacred historical object has hardly dimmed despite the development of new means of exact reproduction, the "copy" itself has now also become sanctified. We can already see, in the permutations witnessed since the completion of the Pompidou Center, a clear indication that the form of the new museum is beginning to piece itself together. Within even the most revivalist of shells—Philip Johnson's Museum of Broadcasting, say, or Michael Graves's enlarged revision of the Whitney—the interior spaces, shaped by programmatic directives, bear only incidental relationship to the original (if not the reconditioned) Louvre: that is, to the past.

The rooms, for example, are both larger and smaller—larger to admit an expanded and educated lay audience that dwarfs the old elite, and smaller to admit a whole range of specialized activities and media that demand a personal rather than public presence. Furthermore the new audience expects these media, just as its ancestors expected text beside paintings. As the twentieth century nears its end, an entire generation of schoolchildren has begun to learn about art history through the imagery displayed on computer screens prompted by keyboards that allow precise manipulation of content, not to mention history itself. If we were therefore to list the physical characteristics of the late-twentieth-century museum, we would begin with the chameleon gallery/room/terminal. The "universal" gallery, in other words, dear both to classicists like Durand and hidebound moderns like William Lescaze (who insisted in 1937 that "a rectangular room, about 25 feet in width and at least one and one half times its width in length" was the perfect model[31]) is gone forever. Symmetry, balance, and order are hardly adjectives that can be attributed to

the inner workings of the new museum, however serene the facade that wraps around them.

The presence of electronic media in these rooms—which began to appear as exhibition aids in the 1980s—is an element that seems at once secure in the present and formidably decisive in the future. Traditionalists rarely take television or computer display into architectural account, but their blindness is to be expected, if not accepted. In William Ivins's seminal analysis of the decisive changes brought about in our understanding of art by printmaking and photography, he rails at the refusal of conventional historians to consider the conceptual revolution effected by technical change.[32] In the next century it is virtually impossible to imagine a work of art being mounted in an exhibition without the viewer being given access to a wide range of supplementary information. Museums no longer, therefore, aspire to become encyclopedic treasure houses of the world's original masterpieces. Because the possibilities for instantaneous transmission of visual and textual information are now almost limitless thanks to computer systems of instantaneous retrieval (as the pioneering research of the Smithsonian Institution and the Jean Paul Getty Museum has proven)[33] each museum is now potentially every museum.

When the Hirshhorn Museum's Stephen Weil speaks of the thickening texture of contemporary life,[34] he is referring to much more than the web of social, political, and financial arrangements that bind us from birth to death. He means as well the complex interactions that characterize commerce and the culture of public life, in the center of which the museum operates as a civic center or town square. It is no accident that the immense central corridor of Edward Larrabee Barnes's Dallas Mu-

seum is its most memorable feature, as are the transparent cylindrical staircases that enfold the Pompidou Center. The treasure house is now a form of urban thoroughfare, a fact that architects have begun to acknowledge explicitly in grand entrance hall after entrance hall. We now expect to be saluted, if not overpowered, inside the door of every museum.

Cesar Pelli's maligned escalators at MOMA recognize this contemporary social reality, as does Parc de la Villette, the witty cultural pasture erected by Bernard Tschumi in Paris in 1989 with galleries, restaurants, and boutiques scattered about the green landscape like fragments torn from an early cubist collage. Christopher Lasch, in his famous indictment of the post–Vietnam War generation, *The Culture of Narcissism*, ignores this intricate homogenizing function. Lamenting the loss of community with the decline of political parties and churches, Lasch fails to recognize their replacement by a complex of vibrant cultural forms, which include popular films, music, fashion—and certainly the museum, the latest house of contemporary worship. The grand staircase, the broad walkable corridors, the honeycombed asymmetrical galleries, and of course the elegant theaters and restaurants are the obvious interior elements that define the potential of the "next" museum, as the exteriors of nearly all the museums examined in this book do not. The space or studio left "open" to the on-site creation of the work of art itself is a subtler but

171

*Bernard Tschumi
Associates.
Parc de la Villette,
Paris. Interior of
Folie L5.*

172

*Bernard Tschumi
Associates.
Parc de la Villette,
Paris. Folie L5.*

173

*Eisenman Architects.
Wexner Center for the
Visual Arts,
Ohio State University,
Columbus, Ohio.
Aerial View.*

174

*Eisenman Architects.
Wexner Center for the
Visual Arts,
Ohio State University,
Columbus, Ohio.
Side view of entrance.*

171

172

173

174

equally radical element that has begun to appear in these later decades. When Ohio State University in Columbus embarked upon a national competition for an architect to expand its art gallery in 1983, it pointedly demanded spaces where the treasures of the past could be augmented by contemporary artistic production. New York architect Peter Eisenman and the Columbus combine of Richard Trott and James H. Bean, the victorious designers of what was later named the Wexner Center for the Visual Arts, responded by providing a transparent skin around large, open, malleable spaces that could be converted, in their own words, into "avant-garde or unconventional galleries . . . with art/ viewer relationships yet to be discovered." The long, low, north-south spine that contains the bulk of the Wexner's galleries is covered with a gridded metal-and-glass envelope. Situated in the center of the campus, the spine weaves through a dense package of buildings and is tracked by a corridor that guarantees the daily passage of thousands of students. At every step, the Wexner reveals both to its interior and exterior audience the full range of its activity, from the traditional exhibition to the on-site work of its artists-in-residence.

Though its architects prefer to characterize the Wexner's spine as a "void," rather than a "solid"—as an absence of signification or metaphor rather than its imposition—it seems to connote a shift in the purpose of all museums, particularly those of the future. The Wexner's use of a transparent skin of glass and of the neutral, machine-age geometry of the modernist grid is particularly apt. Here is a museum that calls attention to its contents as a program or process rather than a static archive. The see-through spine by which it attempts to court the entire public rather than simply those who enter its halls is yet another critical distinction. Given the two enormous changes that have affected all museum design in recent decades—the expansion of the educated audience and the dimunition of rare, available masterpieces—the Wexner's spine is an evocative symbol of the times.

175

176

177

178
Norman Foster,
Foster Associates.
Mediathèque Gallery,
Nîmes, France.
Longitudinal section.

The Future Perfect: Tense

I am far from an approach that says style is first, that tries to do the same thing as done before. For me, every job is an adventure.
—Renzo Piano, interview (1987)

The culture of critical discourse (CCD) is an historically evolved set of rules, a grammar of discourse. . . . It is a culture of discourse in which there is nothing that speakers will on principle permanently refuse to discuss or make problematic; indeed, they are even willing to talk about the value of talk itself and its possible inferiority to silence or to practice.
—Alvin Gouldner, The Future of Intellectuals and the Rise of the New Class *(1979)*

The "styles" employed on the surface of museums erected since the Pompidou Center are considerably less interesting and provocative than the elements of their interiors. Inspired by its origins as a royal palace, the museum has consistently attempted to refer back to an elitist past even as it has courted the support of the mass public. Though the extraordinary exteriors designed by Richard Meier for Atlanta's High Museum and James Stirling for the Staatsgalerie in Stuttgart point to formidable formal achievements, their references are indisputably backward, paying homage to a time when the notion of art as discourse or experience (or least of all as non-object) was an alien one. Informed by Robert Venturi's early, often misunderstood theories—which led to the brief explosion of the pseudorevivalist postmodern style of the 1970s and early 1980s—the architects who reaffirmed the "imperial" museum in these years were equally committed to the contradiction of providing revisionist functions within. The postmodern museum may in fact be considered a relic of its particular time, a period style without serious reference to the evolution of museum design except for its extraordinary interior spaces.

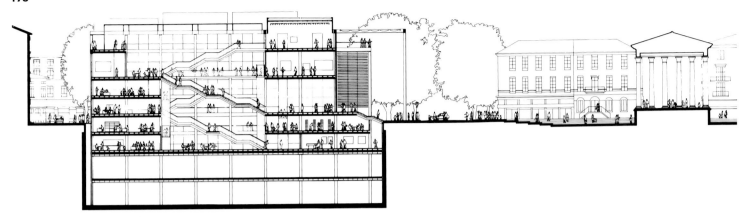

Of course there are exceptions. Museums like Renzo Piano's Menil Collection, Norman Foster's Mediathèque in Nîmes, France, and the Wexner in Columbus, Ohio, all explicitly recognize in varying ways the new conditions under which they must function—at once as archive, laboratory for the new, and city square. Each of these structures also responds in quite specific ways to the site and place in which it rises, and it is precisely this combination of specificity and open neutrality that characterizes virtually all of the museums that are responsive to our lives here at the end of century.

Piano's comfortable steel-and-glass townhouse, sheathed in gray-stained heart of cypress planks, refers, as we have noted, to the area in which it resides. The Mediathèque, designed by British architect Norman Foster for the ancient Roman city of Nîmes, gestures directly across the town's central square to the ancient town hall, the Maison Carré. While the Mediathèque resembles its neighbor in exterior form and dimension, it maintains a clear reference, in its sleek transparent facade topped by an immense light funnel on its roof, to its programmatic emphasis on film and video. The Wexner's radical, gridded spine is fronted by a reinterpreted reconstruction of an old, half-remembered redbrick armory that had been destroyed by fire near the site. At the entrance, then, the Wexner reminds visitors not of a grand abstract past but of local context—before confronting them with the endless, capacious options that lie ahead.

These museums build a conceptual paradigm that avoids simpleminded revivalism. They bring into evidence qualities that have been woven into the fabric of many extraordinary structures planned or finished near the end of this century. José Rafael Moneo's Museum of Roman Art in Mérida shares this specificity of reference to site and use. Richard Meier's sprawling Jean Paul Getty Center in Los Angeles, in which a string of stone-covered buildings are clustered along two diagonals created by the site's intersecting mountain ranges, reveals a similar determination to embrace the contours of its own place; indeed the landscape itself determines the placement and the dimensions of each structure. Emilio Ambasz, whose equally reverent Lucille Halsell Observatory near San Antonio, Texas, presents a series of clear glass pyramids, cones, and conic sections nestled deep into the side of a green hill, buries this museum of organic parts within the earth that provides its very content. Inside each of these clear globes, the visitor, who descends into the space from above ground, finds rare trees, flowers, fauna, and exhibitions in an environment carefully controlled and guarded against the burning Texas sun.

In totally different contexts—and on different scales—the renovations and extensions planned for sites as dissimilar as

179

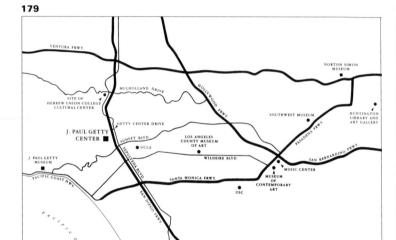

180

181

179
*Map showing
location of
J. Paul Getty Center,
Los Angeles.*

180
*Richard Meier &
Partners.
J. Paul Getty Center,
Los Angeles.
Model of site plan.*

181
*Norman Foster,
Foster Associates.
Mediathèque Gallery,
Nîmes, France.
Model showing Maison
Carré.*

182
*Emilio Ambasz &
Associates.
Lucile Halsell Conser-
vatory at the San An-
tonio Botanical Garden
Center, San Antonio,
Texas.*

182

183

184

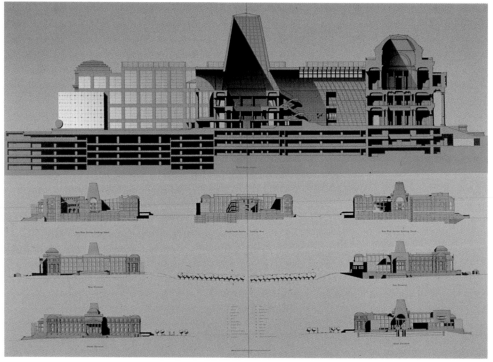

Brooklyn and Montreal betray a similar paradigm. The ambitious plan for the Brooklyn Museum by Arata Isozaki and James Polshek, which came together under the pressure of yet another international competition, refers faithfully to the historical and contemporary complex that lies at the heart of this valiant institution's attempt to resurrect its early glory. With the Brooklyn Museum, originally planned by the firm of McKim, Mead, and White as the world's largest museum, covering 1,500,000 square feet of neoclassical space, Brooklyn limped toward the century's end on less than a fourth of McKim's structure, and that part now badly in need of repair. Isozaki and Polshek envision not only restoration, particularly of the grand staircase excised by zealous simplifiers in 1934, but the creation of an entirely new wing as well as other structures that would surround two sculpture courts and reorient the museum toward the park and its verdant eastern side. Though the new wing gently echoes the Beaux-Arts limestone of the original structure, it harbors two defiantly modern galleries clad in titanium and marked by rotating cube forms located to the southwest and southeast corners. Hovering over this variegated 681,500-square-foot mix of times and tenses towers a 150-foot-high truncated obelisk, an ironic replacement for the arch originally created by McKim, Mead, and White and one that gestures directly to the collection itself, in which the artifacts of Egyptian art remain supreme.

185

186

Peter Rose.
Canadian Centre
for Architecture,
Montreal.
Facade and entrance.

187

Peter Rose.
Canadian Centre
for Architecture,
Montreal.
Library.

188

Peter Rose.
Canadian Centre
for Architecture,
Montreal.
Library.

187

188

189

Peter Rose.
Canadian Centre
for Architecture,
Montreal.
Gallery installation

190

Fumihiko Maki
and Associates.
Spiral Building,
Tokyo, Japan.
Facade.

The Isozaki-Polshek plan is an open mixture of brutal, even primal, modern forms and references to, if not repetitions of, the museum's neoclassical past. The Canadian Centre for Architecture in Montreal by Peter Rose, assisted by his patron Phyllis Lambert (who recommended Mies van der Rohe to her father in 1958 and thus made possible the historic Seagram Building in New York) is an even tougher mixture of disparate parts. This broad, U-shaped structure is formed in three parts—two wings centered on an old structure from 1874 called the Shaugnessy House. When Lambert purchased the plot and decided to create one of the world's first full-scale museums devoted entirely to architecture, she had urged her architect to save the old gray limestone mansion despite its ungainly features. Rose masterfully flanked the old house with wings that gently repeat the old brickwork but with different patterns, notches, and edges. Rose also turned attention away from the front of the old house by 180 degrees, routing the public into the museum through a new, parallel facade that fronts the park, not the street, and whose rusticated base, ornamental metal stripping, and white aluminum-framed windows subtly mark the modernity of the building.

Inside, the Canadian Centre is the antithesis of the classical Durand ideal, with libraries, public halls, study rooms, auditoriums, offices, and vaults, each one fine-tuned to light, climate, and context. Indeed the multiplicity of its functions defines the center, just as it does at the Wexner, the Mediathèque in Nîmes, and the Menil. Here is an institution that knows no suitable name, one that practices at once collection, storage, exhibition, research, and education, and that takes an activist role in conservation in Montreal and beyond.

Then what indeed is a "museum" in the late twentieth century? Almost a hundred years ago, the American Association of Museums defined it simply as "a public institution in which private cultural treasure is displayed and explained for the common good."[35] But those were days when neither architect nor client dared to mix what seemed to be separate functions—a form of abstinence clearly foreign to virtually all those "museums" discussed in this chapter. Fumihiko Maki's elegant

189

191

191

*Fumihiko Maki
and Associates.
Spiral Building,
Tokyo, Japan.
Interior, ground floor
with staircase.*

192

*Fumihiko Maki
and Associates.
Spiral Building,
Tokyo, Japan.
Interior, view of
restaurant.*

192

193

Spiral Building in the heart of Tokyo is perhaps the most dramatic example of the hermaphroditic animal that the house of culture has become. Containing an art gallery, cafes, restaurants, boutiques, offices, and meeting rooms, the Spiral Building is an active, multiform art center. Maki's facade is itself a collage of extremes, mixing geometric forms reminiscent of the early moderns with a cone that remarks playfully on the profession of his client (a lingerie manufacturer). Inside, the entrance lobby provides a semi-cylindrical, four-story courtlike interior flooded with sun from a skylight above that is poised at the head of a gently curved spiral staircase. Lavishly appointed with gleaming metals and works of art tucked into virtually every corner, the Spiral Building is a mirror of its contradictory time and of art's place in a society irretrievably torn between the ideals of sanctity and pagan pleasure.

Since this book charts the shift of architectural focus and practice away from the museum-as-temple and toward a broader, more complex set of functions, it is tempting to speculate about the end, in every sense, of the change. If we cannot imagine a time when no one will be interested in building or extending museums of art, science, or history, neither could priests and parishioners imagine the end of church building barely one century ago. Yet we rear no cathedrals now, at least not on the magnificent scale that once was common. Values, clearly, have shifted. The need to pray, to worship, to seek com-

munion in religion has been replaced at least in part by the need to behold original objects of art and culture, to debate their relative importance, and to stay in contact with our colleagues and neighbors.

But surely this might change. If Alvin Gouldner is correct, if the central focus of the educated masses in postindustrial society is on *discourse* rather than icon or object, conceivably the time may come when the art museum—if not the museum devoted to science or history—may seem an anomaly. Funds may dry up, the buildings themselves fall into disrepair, and the public may dwindle. Or perhaps (and we can see the early signs of this now) the work of "art," or indeed the entire history of art, may come to content itself with non-material expression, in the form of video or a computer disc.

Will the museum, then, be emptied of its physical contents, as the houses of worship have been emptied, and the railroad stations before them? If its vast halls become employed for other, certainly public uses, what manner of events will take place there? No one can now say, just as the architect of the Louvre or his client the king could not have guessed that building's final destiny as the public meeting ground of painting and sculpture. The future of function is beyond our prediction. But certainly we can say that the formal glory of these buildings will survive the death of the museum as admirably as they have augmented its thriving, present-day life.

193
*Fumihiko Maki
and Associates.
Spiral Building,
Tokyo, Japan.
Interior.*

Afterword THE BILLION-DOLLAR PAINTING
AND BEYOND

194

Picasso's Au Lapin
Agile *on the block at
Sotheby's in 1989 —
the painting sold for
$40.7 million to the
Walter Annenberg
Collection, Rancho
Mirage, California.*

. . . .

We have to get used to another higher level of art prices.
—Thomas Ammann, Zürich dealer (1988)

All of this would seem to sound the death knell for museum buying, which, except for a few exceptions, has not been competitive with private initiatives for some time.
—Thomas Messer, director, Guggenheim Museum, letter to author (1988)

In the history of human culture it is very hard to think of any other behavioral system of comparable elaboration and no apparent practical utility that has ever developed even once.
—Joseph Alsop, The Rare Art Traditions: The History of Art Collecting and Its Linked Phenomena (1982)

The quantitative expansion of the museum in the twentieth century has raised profound qualitative questions about its role and its destiny. Due to the unprecedented rise in the cost of the commodity it pretends to contain, the art museum is particularly threatened. The skyrocketing value of those works of art certified by art historians, by public exhibition, and finally by public auction, calls into doubt the museum's function as the final repository of the fine and high arts. Centuries ago, when the realm of the muses or *Mouseion* was primarily the domain of the heads of state or wealthy nobles who commissioned the works kept there, quantification of value played a small role. The very idea of "art," linked to notions of divine inspiration, betrays these non-secular origins. By the end of the nineteenth century, however, democratic revolutions, the Enlightenment, and the growth of widespread bourgeois wealth permanently revised the status of the artist and his work. From the moment when French revolutionaries opened the official salons, saluting the free, unfettered spirit of individual talent ("Independence," said the official catalog of 1793, "is the property of Genius"[36]) to the moment in the eighteenth century when public exhibitions in public galleries began to certify artworks on the basis of broad general appeal (infuriating aristocratic intellectuals like Goethe), art gained the potential to become as material in its essence as gold, frankincense, or myrrh.

In this century the process has quickened, giving rise on the one hand to exhilaration among those who see the steadily rising price of art as an index of heightened cultivation in the public at large, and inspiring profound disgust among those who see the work of art as a fragile representation of humanity's highest achievements, best protected and preserved in institutions that encourage its study or observation. This tension between two entirely opposite points of view explains why the spectacle of the public art auction appears to its audience at once as Paradise and Armageddon.

The sale of almost any work of painting, sculpture, photography, furniture, or crockery made or "touched" by an artist of distinction routinely exceeds its estimate by two or three times. The thoroughly mundane cookie jars once collected by Andy Warhol, auctioned at Sotheby's in 1988, are a perfect example. Buyers and gawkers routinely gasp at Sotheby's on these occasions, some in horror, some in ecstatic approval. In the late eighties an undistinguished Pollock called *Search* fetched twice the amount paid by the National Gallery of Australia in 1973 for *Blue Poles*, a far stronger work, and from the start of the transaction to its finish, both sides vigorously shook their heads—either vertically or horizontally. When younger artists with minimal exhibition records began to post enormous prices as well (Mark Tansey, for example, who sold a freshly finished figurative painting for $190,000 at Sotheby's in 1988 through the catalog displaying nothing but a working drawing[37]), entrepreneurs applauded while traditionalists groaned, deeply.

Critics and historians of museology as well as architecture have preferred to dismiss these events, to assume that the situation is simply a commercial one that will not affect the greater culture, and in particular the community that makes, judges, and exhibits the works that fetch one record price after another. Yet it appears that these records are inseparable from the exchange between art and the public in the modern and postmodern period. Records are set almost every season for prices paid for a work of sculpture, for a work by a living American artist, for works of individual artists such as Pollock, Giacometti, Franz Kline, Cy Twombly, Richard Estes, or Wayne Thiebaud—to mention just a few artists who set precedents in the spring of 1988. A lamp by Frank Lloyd Wright purchased for pennies at an antique store in 1964 brought $704,000 at auction that same year, and the record for the amount spent at auction on contemporary art rose into the tens of millions—a limit repeatedly surpassed with every passing year.

In the midst of the most quantified era in human history, when figures are compiled and stored on every aspect of work, love, and life, art has become one of the most quantified—and perhaps the most expensive of quantities. No shift of such a magnitude can fail to carry nonmaterial implications. Of course the making and meaning of art has been transformed, as Goethe and others foresaw. The auction system at Christie's and Sotheby's manipulates artists as well as objects, and with them the curators, critics, historians, and journalists who analyze the objects. The notion that art is precious but fragile, somehow above the world, beautiful but useless, like a flower in a field, has cracked, out front in the world, if not back in the universities where Plato maintains his hold. The first message of this Afterword, for both designers and managers of museums (as well as the public), is unmistakable: *get ready*.

The Platonists and their allies will object. How can *art*, this nonfunctional commodity, be reduced to such crass quantification by the vulgar society that surrounds it? Consider the following: as the year 2000 approaches, art has risen in value to the point where it has surpassed life and almost rivals death. Sold for $4.8 million in 1988, Jackson Pollock's unimpressive *Search* was four to five times as dear as an artificial heart. Even in the future, when the artificial heart may be perfected and offer exceptionally prolonged life, any major Pollock will still cost more. If the total value of the May 1988, Sotheby's contemporary art auction was only one-third that of the Pentagon building ($83 million in 1943), we must remember that art rises rather than depreciates in value, unlike most architecture and certainly unlike the Pentagon. *Search* alone appreciated 2,400 percent between its sale at auction for $200,000 in 1971 and for $4.8 million in 1988. The rate of increase for *Blue Poles* between 1956, when it sold for $6,000, and 1973, when the Australians bought it came to 50,000 percent, a figure that suggests that *Poles* should be worth $1 billion by the fall of 1997. Now it just so happens that a B-1 bomber cost precisely $1 billion in the 1980s, meaning that certain masterpieces let loose at auction (*Blue Poles*, say, or the *Mona Lisa*) would equal the cost of at least one of the major instruments of modern destruction.

During this period only the cost of the MX missile appears to have outdone that of art: the program to build the missile cost the taxpayer approximately $40 billion per year. But art's weakness in the face of the gross defense budget is only temporary—remember its potential to rise, not fall, in value. In the year 2008, the Edgar Degas sculpture *Little Dancer at Fourteen Years of Age*, which recently fetched a record-breaking $10.12 million at auction, will still be soaring, worth at least $1,023,117,417, while America's MX missiles will be rusting away somewhere, replaced by a neo-MX. Already as costly as life, art may yet prove as imperious and vulgar as death.

Or it may not. There are no real historical precedents for what we witnessed as the twentieth century neared its close. Though there have been periods when stunning prices have been paid by kings and merchants for single works of art—the elector of Saxony astonished the world in 1754, for example, when he paid £8,500 for Raphael's Sistine *Madonna*—there is no period that rivals ours for sheer expenditure. The number of corporate and individual bidders prepared to spend well into the millions has taken a quantum leap, as any auctioneer or dealer you happen to question will tell you. Certainly we are not prepared on any ethical, critical, or theoretical level for these numbers. But we must begin to assess the impact of art's price on a wide range of hitherto sacrosanct issues—including the sanctity of art itself.

I saw gem stones [at the Warhol] auction that he bought from me for $300 sell for $10,000, and they were only quartz.
—Vito Giallo, antiques dealer, interview (1988)

Money is less expensive than immortality.
—Eugene M. Schwartz, collector, interview (1988)

Classical Dross

The argument can be made that the sale of the Warhol collection of kitsch was moved by considerations beyond beauty. Except for an occasional Art Deco vase, a glittering old automobile, a Twombly, perhaps a Lichtenstein, we saw nothing but dross— classically considered—at Sotheby's. But the eager crowds and consortium of buyers bidding for cookie jars were not seeking craftsmanship or inspiration. What they reached for was the apparent transcendence summed up in that fatal word "artist." It is this transcendence that explains why collectors increasingly unload lavish sums for works of art that are fragile, ugly (by almost anyone's standards), or almost impossible to preserve, as is the case with certain photographs, videotapes, and films. Van Gogh's *Sunflower*, bought for $19.8 million in 1987, is as faded and imperiled as the steadily darkening *Mona Lisa* at the Louvre or Julian Schnabel's heavy, decomposing canvases, from which dishes drop and shatter with alarming regularity. When approached at a gallery, British artist David Hockney immediately agreed that no one knew how long his collages of SX-70 Polaroid snapshots would last. "Maybe only a few years," he said, smiling. Naturally they continue to command imposing prices in private and public sales. Clearly these objects are less important as concrete works of art than for the status they have been accorded by art history and by legend.

In the cases of Warhol, Schnabel, Hockney, and many others, the contemporary bourgeois collector is attracted, not repelled, by the contemporaneity of the work. In contrast, consider the response of the European art market in the mid-seventeenth century to the massive sale of King Charles I's royal collection by the Puritan rulers of England, at least the equal of Warhol at Sotheby's. The freshly beheaded king's holdings included 400 pieces of sculpture and more than 1,400 paintings, including Raphaels, Michelangelos, Titians, Dürers, Holbeins, and Rembrandts. Though some of the king's horse trappings fetched higher prices than his art, most of the works sold for respectable prices except the contemporary works. Three Rembrandts, for example, went for exactly £5 apiece.

What was missing in the market for Charles I's collection was the leisured middle class, which hangs now on every rumor, every nuance, every review written in every magazine and periodical published anywhere. The buyers then were court emissaries, for the most part. Kings, queens, dukes, and duchesses wanted only certain coin of the realm, not Rembrandts, which were hardly known or trumpeted in their day in the manner that Hockney is in ours. Call it critical mass if you will. Call it an audience of millions compared to an audience of hundreds. But there you have it.

Art-as-Barter

The second message of this afterword is: over the long run Floyd is right and Feigen is wrong. Certain artists may fade, and the market itself may rise or fall with the state of the economy. But the marketing system now in place is anchored in the center, not the margin, of society, and it is therefore secure. In the sense that it implies the collapse of the contemporary art economy, then, Feigen's readjustment of value will never take place. If pop art fades, minimalism rises to replace it. If neo-expressionism pales, neo-geo is invented. Barely dry paintings by Tansey and others sold at auction may be setting new records for the speed of their public acceptance, but the concept of *immediate history* is suggested on virtually every level of the new marketing system. Following the lead of museums eager to embrace the next stage of evolution, collectors no longer feel the necessity to wait. Auction purchase itself now confers validation. And collectors beget collectors, who beget, indeed often invent, new art movements to patronize.

Nor is any particular political system, medium, or strategy beyond the scope of the system. Once thought resistant to art-as-barter, both the U.S.S.R. and China have begun to schedule auctions at which their living artists hawk their works before capitalists on tour in Moscow and Beijing. And photography, once deemed uncollectible because of its easy reproducibility, is now as common to the auction halls as a still-life painting. Even conceptual art was ingested with ease by this voracious market, and in its least accommodating forms. Collector Gilbert Silverman of Detroit bid $90,000 for Hans Haacke's *Social Grease* in 1987 without the slightest hesitation, though the work overtly mocks six major corporate and political figures (including David Rockefeller, Douglas Dillon, and Richard Nixon) by quoting each of them on a separate metal plaque advocating support of the arts as a "social lubricant."

There is nothing which is faintly artistic that we wouldn't sell.
—John Floyd, chairman, Christie's, interview (1988)

The buying of contemporary art is definitely linked to the financial market. [It] has nothing to do with art. . . . But something will change. Contemporary art is overvalued. I can't tell you when the readjustment is coming but it is coming. There will be a readjustment of price to value.
—Richard Feigen, dealer, interview (1988)

The Remote Present

On one level, the quantitative revolution—of people and dollars—appears to sound the death knell for those museums intent on building a serious collection. The relentless approach of the multi-billion dollar work of art, driven by the expansion of the market and by its ability to subsume almost any new movement; the continued creation of new museums that increase the number of bidders for "masterpieces" (an almost weekly occurrence, according to some authorities); and the dwindling availability of Giottos, Rembrandts, and Pollocks—all of this adds up to a deadlock. One symbol of this condition might well be the empty storage towers of Kenzo Tange's Municipal Museum in Yokohama. Rising before the Pacific where Admiral Perry sailed in from the west in the nineteenth century, Tange's is an empty museum with no past to preserve, restore, or praise.

But the assumption that it must remain empty presumes that the objects we prize are few in number and circumscribed by the past. Left no alternative, we can expect that institutions like Yokohama might turn to the acquisition and display of contemporary art, the production of which by any standard is massive. But only a fraction of the more than one billion objects now owned by American museums are traditional works of art. Faced with the rapid replacement of tools, clothes, and entire life-styles by mercurial social and political forces, our museums now seek to preserve the present as well as the past. In Sweden in the 1970s the Nordiska Museum began a wide-ranging program of collecting ordinary household objects each year, documenting the present moment as though it were about to fade into the remoteness of the Middle Ages, as it is.

Postindustrial Platonism

In a postindustrial society in which people and machines are transformed as a matter of course each decade, the museum becomes a means of holding fast to our identity. Commonly considered a symbol of the steady state, the museum in fact attests to ceaseless change. What is fine and high is ironically drawn now from what is low and familiar. But given the escalation in our time of cash, leisure, and art production, the Platonic ideal is certain to flourish rather than falter. Only now can an entire class, floating between poverty and the dream of royalty, afford to pursue the vision defined by Plato and redefined in every classroom we visit. Of course we bid in the auction halls because we are certain that others hold these useless objects in the same esteem that we do. Equally obviously, our errors of judgment will be compounded by the number of artists, collectors, and museums now engaged in this doomed pursuit. Art has never been more vulgar than now because life has never been more vulgar, poised on the edge of self-destruction.

But this is precisely why the price of art knows no limit, why museums abound, why they enfold virtually every sector of our lives, and why they will never lack for objects or mission in our lifetimes. Vulgarity whets the desire for its opposite. We bid for art, more of us than ever before, to escape life. Failing time and again, we keep on paying, in pursuit of a goal that is clearly beyond price.

Whoever shall be guided so far toward the mysteries of love, by contemplating beautiful things rightly in due order is now approaching the last grade. Suddenly he will behold a beauty marvelous in its nature, that very beauty . . . for the sake of which all the earlier hardships had been borne.
—*Plato*, The Symposium

NOTES

1

Helen Searing, "The Development of Museum Typology," in *Building the New Museum*, ed. Suzanne Stephens (New York: The Architectural League of New York/Princeton Architectural Press, 1986), pp. 14–23.

2

William Rubin, "When Museums Overpower Their Own Art," *New York Times*, April 12, 1987, sec. H.

3

Ibid.

4

Nathaniel Burt, *Palaces for the People: A Social History of the American Art Museum* (Boston: Little, Brown & Co., 1977), p. 18.

5

Louis Harris, *Americans and the Arts* (New York, 1975); *Americans and the Arts*, no. 4 (New York: American Council for the Arts, 1984).

6

National Center for Education Statistics with the U.S. Department of Education, Museum Program Survey (Washington, D.C., 1979), p. 10.

7

Charles Rosen and Henri Zerner, *Romanticism and Realism: The Mythology of Nineteenth-Century Art* (New York: Viking Press, 1984). Douglas Davis, "The Avant-Garde Is Dead! Long Live the Avant-Garde!" *Art in America* 20, no. 4 (April 1982): 9–17.

8

Roger Milles, "Museum Audiences," *International Journal of Museum Management and Curatorship* 5, no. 1 (March 1986): 73–80.

9

In Stephens, ed., *Building the New Museum*, p. 84.

10

Joseph Wright Alsop, *The Rare Art Traditions: The History of Art Collecting and Its Linked Phenomena Wherever These Have Appeared* (New York: Harper & Row, 1982), pp. 93–95.

11

Carol Duncan and Alan Wallach, "The Universal Survey Museum," *Art History* 3, no. 4 (December 1980): 67–71.

12

Richard Rogers, interview with author, London, 1986.

13

Charles Rosen and Henri Zerner, "The Museum of the Century," *New York Review of Books* 23, no. 4 (March 18, 1976): 32–34.

14

Michael Gibson, "Les Visages multiples de Gae Aulenti," *Connaissance des Arts* 411 (May 1986): 71–72.

15

Douglas Davis, "Notes for a Prologue to a Decade," *Museum News* 59, no. 1 (January–February 1981): 20–27.

16

Hilton Kramer, *Age of the Avant-Garde* (New York: Farrar, Straus & Giroux, 1972), p. 39.

17

Kozo Okudaira, "History of Museum Architecture," in *Japanese Museum Architecture*, ed. Seiji Oshima (Tokyo: Setagaya Art Museum, 1987), pp. 163–70.

18

Hiroshi Sasaki, "The Museum Boom in Japan," *Process Architecture*, no. 28 (March 1982): 17.

19

Fumihiko Maki, "The Public Dimension in Contemporary Architecture," in *New Public Architecture: Recent Projects by Fumihiko Maki and Arata Isozaki* (New York: Japan Society, 1985), p. 16.

20

Thomas Leavitt, *Future Directions for Museums of American Art* (Fort Worth: Amon Carter Museum of Western Art, 1980), p. 25.

21

Cesar Pelli, interview with the author, New Haven, Conn., May 14, 1988.

22

Francis Haskell, "The Artist and the Museum," *New York Review of Books* 34, no. 24 (December 3, 1987): 41.

23

William S. Rubin, *Dada and Surrealist Art* (New York: Harry N. Abrams, 1968), p. 37.

24

A. A. Bronson and Peggy Gale, eds., *Museums by Artists* (Toronto: Art Metropole, 1983), p. 10.

25

"Isamu Noguchi's Garden Museum," *Promenade* (April–September 1988): 76.

26

Bronson and Gale, *Museums by Artists*, p. 76.

27

Herbert Distel, *The Museum of Drawers* (Zurich: Kunsthaus Zurich, 1978), p. 12.

28

Philip Johnson in Museum of Broadcasting press release on the occasion of the unveiling of Johnson's model and plan, 1988.

29

Christian Norberg-Schulz, "The Demand for a Contemporary Language of Architecture," *Art and Design* 2 (December 1986): 20.

30

Sidney Tillim, "Benjamin Rediscovered: The Work of Art after the Age of Mechanical Reproduction," *Artforum* 21, no. 5 (May 1983): 67–73.

31

William Lescaze, "A Modern Housing for a Museum," *Parnassus* 9, no. 6 (November 1937): 42.

32

William Ivins, *Prints and Visual Communication* (Cambridge, Mass.: Harvard University Press, 1953), p. 180.

33

Joel N. Bloom, Ellen Cochran Hicks, Mary Ellen Munley, and Earl A. Powell III, *Museums for a New Century* (Washington, D.C.: American Association of Museums, 1984), p. 47.

34

Stephen Weil, *Beauty and the Beasts: On Museums, Art, the Law, and the Market* (Washington, D.C.: Smithsonian Institution Press, 1983), p. 89.

35

Bloom et al, *Museums for a New Century*, p. 55.

36

Elizabeth Gilmore Holt, ed., "Official Catalogue: Salon of Year II (1793)," *The Triumph of Art for the Public: The Emerging Role of Exhibitions and Critics* (Garden City, N.Y.: Anchor Press, 1979), p. 46.

37

Stephen Weil, "Enough Museums?" *ArtNews* 82, no. 10 (December 1983): 27.

BIBLIOGRAPHY

Books

Alexander, Steven, and Eugene Diserio, eds. *Rooms P. S. 1*. New York: Institute of Art and Urban Resources, 1977.

Alsop, Joseph. *The Rare Art Traditions: The History of Art Collecting and Its Linked Phenomena Wherever These Have Appeared*. New York: Harper & Row, 1982.

Amon Carter Museum of Western Art. *Future Directions for Museums of American Art*. Fort Worth: Amon Carter Museum of Western Art, 1980.

Apple, Jackie, ed. *Alternatives in Retrospect: An Historical Overview, 1969–1975*. New York: New Museum, 1981.

Arnell, Peter, and Ted Bickford, eds. *Frank Gehry: Buildings and Projects*. New York: Rizzoli International, 1985.

————. *A Center for the Visual Arts: The Ohio State University Competition*. New York: Rizzoli International, 1984.

Baudrillard, Jean. "The Ecstasy of Communication." Translated by Chris Turner. Paris: Editions Galilee, 1987.

Bell, Daniel. *The Coming of Post-Industrial Society*. New York: Basic Books, 1973.

Bloom, Joel N., et al, eds. *Museums for a New Century*. Washington, D.C.: American Association of Museums, 1984.

Book, Jack, ed. *Collecion Panza*. Madrid: Centro de Arte Reina Sofia, 1988.

Brawne, Michael. *The Museum Interior*. New York: Architectural Book Publishing, 1982.

Bronson, A. A., and Peggy Gale, eds. *Museums by Artists*. Toronto: Art Metropole, 1983.

Burt, Nathaniel. *Palaces for the People: A Social History of the American Art Museum*. Boston: Little, Brown & Co., 1977.

Conrads, Ulrich, ed. *Programs and Manifestoes on Twentieth-Century Architecture*. Translated by Michael Bullock. Cambridge: MIT Press, 1970.

Cook, John W. *Conversations with Architects*. New York: Praeger Publishers, 1973.

Darragh, Joan, and Roth Leland, eds. *A New Brooklyn Museum: The Master Plan Competition*. New York: Rizzoli International, 1988.

Denvir, Bernard. *The Impressionists at First Hand*. New York: Thames & Hudson, 1987.

Diamonstein, Barbaralee. *Buildings Reborn: New Uses, Old Places*. New York: Harper & Row, 1978.

Dimaggio, Paul. *Audience Studies of the Performing Arts and Museums*. Washington, D.C.: National Endowment for the Arts, 1978.

Distel, Herbert. *The Museum of Drawers*. Zurich: Kunsthaus Zurich, 1978.

Douglas, Mary, ed. *Rules and Meanings*. London: Penguin, 1977.

Draper, Linda. *The Visitor and the Museum*. Washington, D.C.: American Association of Museums Education Committee, 1977.

Economic Impact of Arts and Cultural Institutions. Washington, D.C.: National Endowment for the Arts, 1981.

Evans, Catherine Inbusch, and Marjorie Munsterberg. *Centre Canadien d'Architecture/Canadian Centre for Architecture: 1979–1984*. Translated by André Bernier. New York: Callaway Editions, 1982.

Gilman, Benjamin Ives. *Museum Ideals of Purpose and Method*. 2d ed. Cambridge, Mass.: Riverside Press, 1923.

Glusberg, Jorge, ed. *Vision of the Modern*. New York: Callaway Editions, 1988.

Gouldner, Alvin W. *The Future of Intellectuals and the Rise of the New Class*. New York: Seabury Press, 1979.

Gropius, Walter. *The New Architecture and the Bauhaus*. Translated by P. Morton Shand. London: Faber & Faber, 1935.

Haigh, Robert W., George Gerbner, and Richard B. Byrne, eds. *Communications in the Twenty-first Century*. New York: John Wiley & Sons, 1981.

Harris, Louis. *Americans and the Arts*. New York: American Council for the Arts, 1975.

Heiss, Alanna, ed. *The Institute for Art and Urban Resources Inc.: P. S. 1: The Clocktower*. New York: John Wiley & Sons, 1981.

Hitchcock, Henry Russell, and Philip Johnson. *The International Style*. 2d ed. New York: W. W. Norton, 1966.

Holt, Elizabeth Gilmore, ed. *The Art of All Nations: 1850–1873*. Garden City, N.Y.: Anchor Press, 1981.

————. *The Triumph of Art for the Public*. Garden City, N.Y.: Anchor Press, 1979.

Hudson, Kenneth. *Museums of Influence: The Pioneers of the Last Two Hundred Years*. New York: Cambridge University Press, 1987.

Ivins, William M. *Prints and Visual Communication*. Cambridge: Harvard University Press, 1953.

Jencks, Charles. *Free-Style Classicism*. New York: St. Martin's Press, 1982.

————. *The Language of Post-Modern Architecture*. New York: Rizzoli International, 1977.

————. *Post-Modernism: The New Classicism in Art and Architecture*. New York: Rizzoli International, 1987.

Johnson, Eugene J., ed. *Charles Moore: Buildings and Projects, 1941–1986*. New York: Rizzoli International, 1986.

Johnson, Philip C. *Mies van der Rohe*. New York: Museum of Modern Art, 1978.

Klotz, Heinrich. *New Museum Buildings in the Federal Republic of Germany*. New York: Rizzoli International, 1985.

Knight, Carleton. *Philip Johnson/John Burgee. Architecture, 1979–1985*. New York: Rizzoli International, 1985.

Krauss, Rosalind E. *The Originality of the Avant-Garde and Other Modernist Myths*. Cambridge, Mass.: MIT Press, 1985.

Le Corbusier, and Pierre Jeanneret. *The Decorative Art of Today*. 1925. Reprint. Translated by James Dunnett. Cambridge, Mass.: MIT Press, 1987.

Lippard, Lucy, ed. *Six Years: The Dematerialization of the Art Object from 1966 to 1972*. New York: Praeger Publishers, 1973.

Montaner, Josep, and Jordi Oliveras. *The Museums of the Last Generation*. New York: St. Martin's Press, 1986.

Motherwell, Robert, ed. *The Dada Painters and Poets*. New York: Wittenborn, Schultz, 1951.

Mozuna, Kiko. *The Architecture of Memory*. Tokyo: Parco, 1985.

Naisbitt, John. *Megatrends*. New York: Warner Books, 1982.

New Public Architecture: Recent Projects by Fumihiko Maki and Arata Isozaki. New York: Japan Society, 1985, pp. 16–19.

O'Dohery, Brian, ed. *Museums in Crisis*. New York: George Braziller, 1972.

Oshima, Seiji. *Japanese Museum Architecture*. Tokyo: Setagaya Arts Museum, 1987.

Pfeiffer, Bruce Brooks. *Frank Lloyd Wright–Guggenheim Correspondence*. Fresno, Calif.: Press at California State University, 1986.

Porphyrios, Demetri. *On the Methodology of Architectural History*. New York: St. Martin's Press, 1981.

Rosen, Charles, and Henri Zerner. *Romanticism and Realism: The Mythology of Nineteenth-Century Art*. New York: Viking Press, 1984.

Rubin, William S. *Dada and Surrealist Art*. New York: Harry N. Abrams, 1968.

Saldern, Axel von. *The Brooklyn Museum: A Handbook*. Brooklyn: Brooklyn Museum, 1967.

Sandler, Irving, and Amy Newman, eds. *Defining Modern Art: Selected Writings of Alfred H. Barr, Jr.* New York: Harry N. Abrams, 1986.

Schinkel, Karl Friedrich. *Sammlung architektonischer Entwurf*. Translated by Karin Cramer. New York: Princeton Architectural Press, 1989.

Searing, Helen. *New American Art Museums*. New York: Whitney Museum of American Art, 1983.

Smithson, Alison, and Peter Smithson. *The Heroic Period of Modern Architecture*. New York: Rizzoli International, 1981.

Stephens, Suzanne, ed. *Building the New Museum*. New York: The Architectural League of New York/Princeton Architectural Press, 1986.

Sudjic, Deyan. *Norman Foster, Richard Rogers, James Stirling: New Directions in British Architecture*. London: Thames & Hudson, 1987.

Thomson, Garry. *The Museum Environment*. London, Boston: Butterworths, 1978.

Venturi, Robert. *Complexity and Contradiction in Architecture*. New York: Museum of Modern Art, 1966.

Weil, Stephen. *Beauty and the Beasts: On Museums, Art, the Law, and the Market*. Washington, D.C.: Smithsonian Institution Press, 1983.

Wingler, Hans M. *The Bauhaus*. Cambridge, Mass.: MIT Press, 1969.

Yankelovich, Daniel. *New Rules*. New York: Random House, 1981.

Zukowsky, John Rizzoli, et al. *Mies Reconsidered: His Career, Legacy, and Disciples*. Chicago: Art Institute of Chicago, 1986.

Baker, Kenneth. "The Saatchi Museum Opens." *Art in America* 73, no. 4 (July 1985): 23–27.

Banham, Reyner. "In the Neighborhood of Art." *Art in America* 75, no. 4 (June 1987): 124–29.

Bell, Jane. "Least Is Most." *Village Voice*, May 8, 1978, p. 26.

Boles, Daralice D. "Accommodating Pope and Pei." *Progressive Architecture* 64, no. 8 (August 1983): 76–79.

Campbell, Robert. "Moore on Moore in Moore." *Architecture* 76, no. 2 (February 1987): 28–39.

Cannon-Brookes, Peter. "Frankfurt and Atlanta: Richard Meier as a Designer of Museums." *Museum Management and Curatorship* 5, no. 1 (March 1986): 39–64.

Davey, Peter, and Dan Cruickshank. "Working with Old Buildings." *Architectural Review* 183, no. 1094 (April 1988): 23–24.

Davis, Douglas. "The Avant-Garde is Dead! Long Live the Avant-Garde!" *Art in America* 20, no. 4 (April 1982): 9–17.

———. "The Death of Semiotics (In Late Modern Architecture); The Corruption of Metaphor (In Post-Modernism); The Birth of the Punctum (In Neo-mania)." *Artforum* 22, no. 9 (May 1984): 56–63.

———. "Late Post-Modern: The End of Style." *Art in America* 75, no. 4 (June 1987): 14–23.

———. "The Museum Impossible." *Museum News* 61, no. 5 (June 1983): 32–37.

———. "Notes for a Prologue to a Decade." *Museum News* 59, no. 1 (January–February 1981): 20–27.

———. "Toward the Billion-Dollar Painting." *Esquire* 43, no. 11 (November 1975): 198–202.

Dean, Andrea Oppenheimer. "The National East: An Evaluation." *Architecture* 73, no. 10 (October 1984): 74–78.

Dimaggio, Paul. "Can Culture Survive the Marketplace?" *Journal of Arts Management and Law* 5, no. 1 (March 1986): 35–37.

Doubilet, Susan. "The Talk of the Town." *Progressive Architecture* 73, no. 10 (October 1984): 74–86.

Duncan, Carol, and Alan Wallach. "The Universal Survey Museum." *Art History* 18, no. 4 (December 1984): 67–71.

Filler, Martin. "Back on Track, Metaphorically Speaking." *Architectural Record* 174, no. 5 (May 1986): 106–13.

Fischer, Volker. "The German Museum of Architecture." *Museum Management and Curatorship* 5, no. 1 (March 1986): 19–26.

Frampton, Kenneth. "The High Museum in Atlanta." *Casabella* 32, no. 11 (November 1982): 50.

Galloway, David. "The New German Museums." *Art in America* 73, no. 7 (July 1985): 74–88.

Gibson, Michael. "Les Visages multiples de Gae Aulenti." *Connaissance des Arts* no. 411 (May 1986): 71–72.

Goldberger, Paul. "Architecture: Museum in Stuttgart Builds a Postmodernist Monument." *New York Times*, April 10, 1985.

———. "In Paris, a Face Lift in Grand Style." *New York Times*, May 17, 1987.

Grove, Richard. "Pioneers in American Museums: John Cotton Dana." *Museum News* 56, no. 3 (May–June 1978): 32–39.

Haskell, Francis. "The Artist and the Museum." *New York Review of Books* 34, no. 24 (December 3, 1987), pp. 41–43.

Hood, Marilyn. "Staying Away: Why People Choose Not to Visit Museums." *Museum News* 61, no. 2 (April 1983): 50–57.

Huet, Bernard. "After the Glorification of Reason." *Lotus International* 8, no. 2 (1986): 209–15.

Huxtable, Ada Louise. "Cultural Shock, Anyone?" *New York Times*, February 13, 1972.

Kadis, Philip M. "Who Should Manage Museums?" *Art News* 76, no. 9 (October 1977): 46.

Katzive, David H. "Museums on the Air." *Museum News* 62, no. 3 (June 1984): 17–18.

Knox, Barbara. "Lighting Design and the Life of Museums." *Architecture* 26, no. 2 (February 1987): 58–59.

Kramer, Hilton. "A New Arts Center in Paris to Open Amid Raging Controversy." *New York Times*, January 30, 1977.

Lescaze, William. "A Modern Housing for a Museum," *Parnassus* 9, no. 6 (November 1937).

McClelland, Andrew L. "The Politics and Aesthetics of Display: Museums in Paris, 1750–1800." *Art History* 7, no. 4 (December 1984).

Magnusson, Emanuela. "Museum Architecture." *Architectural Design* 56, no. 6 (December 1986): 36–40.

Milles, Roger S. "Museum Audiences." *International Journal of Museum Management and Curatorship* 5, no. 1 (March 1986): 73–80.

Miyake, Riichi. "Deconstructivists in Architecture." *Japan Architect* 62, no. 6 (June 1987): 6–9.

Norberg-Schulz, Christian. "The Demand for a Contemporary Language of Architecture." *Art and Design* 2 (December 1986): 14–21.

Papadakis, Dr. Andreas C., ed. "Tate in the North." *Art and Design* 1, no. 3 (April 1985): 50–51.

Pastier, John. "L.A. Art: Dissimilar Duo." *Architecture* 76, no. 2 (February 1987): 40–53.

———. "Simplicity of Form, Ingenuity in the Use of Daylight." *Architecture* 76, no. 5 (May 1987): 84–91.

Rastorfer, Darl. "The Art of Construction." *Architectural Record* 176, no. 1 (January 1988): 103–11.

Rosen, Charles, and Henri Zerner. "The Judgement of Paris." *New York Review of Books* 26, no. 18 (November 22, 1979): 23–25.

———. "The Museum of the Century." *New York Review of Books* 23, no. 4 (March 18, 1976): 32–34.

Rubin, William. "When Museums Overpower Their Own Art." *New York Times*, April 12, 1987.

Sasaki, Hiroshi. "The Museum Boom in Japan." *Process: Architecture* 7, no. 2 (March 1982): 14–18.

Schlereth, Thomas J. "Collecting Today for Tomorrow." *Museum News* 60, no. 2 (March–April 1982): 29–37.

Tillim, Sidney. "Benjamin Rediscovered: The Work of Art after the Age of Mechanical Reproduction." *Art Forum* 21, no. 5 (May 1983).

Tompkins, Calvin. "A Good Monster." *New Yorker* 53, no. 48 (January 16, 1978): 23–26.

Tucker, Paul. "The First Impressionist Exhibition." *Art History* 18, no. 4 (December 1984): 46–50.

Woodbridge, Sally. "The National Museum of Modern Art, Kyoto: Continuity by Contrast." *Japan Architect* 11, no. 2 (March 1987): 35–41.

INDEX

The publisher has made every effort to contact all photographers for correct credits. Any necessary revisions will be included in future editions.

The photographers and sources of photographic material are as follows:

Shigeo Anzai: plates 70–71; © 1990 The Art Institute of Chicago/Thomas Cinoman: plates 133–34; ARTOG/ D. G. Olshavsky: plates 173–77; Daniel Barsotti: plate 47; BLACK STAR, Tom Jacobi/*Stern:* plates 60, 87; © 1987 Michael Bodycomb: plates 53–54; Stuart Brateman: plates 116–17; Richard Bryant/ARCAID: *front cover,* plates 5, 62–63, 88, 89, 90, 92, 108–10, 152, 186–90, 192–93; Centre Canadien d'Architecture, Montreal: plate 161; Kenneth Champlin: plates 136–37; John Cliett: plate 139; Georgio Colombo: plate 154; © Dan Cornish/ESTO: plates 14, 148, 150; George Cott/ CHROMA, Inc.: plate 55; Marliese Darsow: plate 61; Richard Davies: plate 181; Peter A. Davis: plates 143– 44; Herbert Distel: plate 145; Harry A. Dodson: plate 141; Richard Einzig: plate 1; Richard Einzig/ARCAID: plate 25; © Frank O. Gehry & Associates, Inc./Greg Walsh: plates 20, 118–19; Mitumasa Fujizuka: plate 73; Katsuaki Furudate: plates 48, 51, 64–65, 67; Rainer Gaertner: plates 57–59; © Jeff Goldberg/ESTO: plate 166; Hedrich-Blessing: plate 132; Hickey & Robertson, Houston: plates 95–97, 99–100; Greg Hursley, Austin, Tex.: plate 182; Timothy Hursley: plate 121; Yasuhiro Ishimoto: plates 68–69; © 1987 J. Paul Getty Trust and Richard Meier & Partners: plate 180; courtesy John Burgee Architects: plate 167; Toshiharu Kitajima: plates

82, 191; Kishio Kurakawa: plate 75; © Waltraud Krass: plate 122; Robert Lautman for Smithsonian Institution: plates 163–64; Rafael Lobato; plate 155; John Lonat: plate 127; Michael P. McLoughlin: plates 156–58; Marburg/Art Resource, New York: plate 4; Massachusetts Museum of Contemporary Art: plate 140; © Peter Mauss/ESTO: plates 131, 170–72, *back jacket;* courtesy Max Protech Gallery: plate 169; Menil Collection: plate 98; The Metropolitan Museum of Art, New York: plate 126; John Miller/Hedrich-Blessing: plate 130; Michael Moran/Centre Canadien d'Architecture, Montreal: plate 160; Al Mozell: plate 124; Grant Mudford: plates 105–6; Musée d'Orsay, Paris: plates 27–29; © 1990 PHOTO R.M.N.: plates 2, 21, 26, 35–38; © Taisuke Ogawa/SHINKENCHIKU: plates 79–81; Tomio Ohashi: plates 66, 74, 76–78; Pan Image/Robert Schwartz: plate 102; Paschall/Taylor: plate 11; © 1990 Richard Payne, AIA: plate 45; courtesy Pei Cobb Freed & Partners: plates 8–10, 30, 32, 34; Cervin Robinson: plates 7, 135, 138; George Silk: plate 56; © 1990 SITE Projects, Inc.: plate 168; R. D. Smith: plates 93–94; Smithsonian Institution: plates 162, 165; © Ezra Stoller/ ESTO: plates 6, 40–43, 107, 111–15; © Tim Street-Porter: plates 49–50, 52; Gabor Szilasi/Centre Canadien d'Architecture, Montreal: plate 185; William Taylor: plate 13; O. M. Ungers: plate 123; Daniel Varenne, Geneva: plate 142; Virginia Museum of Fine Arts: plates 103–4; Deidi von Schaewen: plate 31; Paul Wakefield: plate 39; Wide World Photo, Inc.: plate 194; Rob Wilson: plates 146–47; Alfred Wolf: plates 3, 17, 33.